Returning to Reality

Returning to Reality

Thomas Merton's Wisdom for a Technological World

Phillip M. Thompson

CASCADE *Books* · Eugene, Oregon

RETURNING TO REALITY
Thomas Merton's Wisdom for a Technological World

Cascade Books
An Imprint of Wipf and Stock Publishers
199 W. 8th Ave., Suite 3
Eugene, OR 97401

www.wipfandstock.com

ISBN 13: 978-1-62032-252-9

Cataloging-in-Publication data:
Thompson, Phillip M.

   Returning to reality : Thomas Merton's wisdom for a technological world / Phillip M. Thompson.

   xxii + 112 p. ; 23 cm. — Includes bibliographical references and index.

   ISBN 13: 978-1-62032-252-9

   1. Merton, Thomas, 1915–1968. 2. Technology. I. Title.

BX4705 .M542 T486 2012

Manufactured in the U.S.A.

Dedicated to my favorite Merton reader, my son, William, who has a keen intellect, a wry sense of humor, and a love of God like Brother Louis.

The way of wisdom is no dream, no temptation and no evasion, for it is on the contrary a return to reality at its very root.

Thomas Merton,
"The Contemplative Life in the Modern World"

Contents

Preface

As I scanned the front page of the *New York Times* one day, I noticed that the lead article was "Growing Up Digital, Wired for Distraction." This article on the "screen generation" detailed how many students could not complete tasks requiring a sustained focus. One bright student who was required to read Kurt Vonnegut's "Cat's Cradle" for school admitted to preferring the "immediate gratification" of YouTube to such reading. On YouTube, the student argued, "You can get a whole story in six minutes."[1] Perhaps, but could you adequately probe the "whole story," exploring the depth and nuance of a sophisticated piece of literature in six minutes? This story is backed by a growing body of social and scientific research that indicates that we are becoming a nation of superficial and distracted consumers of instant messages and images. This growing tendency cannot bode well for religious or other deep commitments that require a sustained level of reflection and contemplation.

There are many other technological issues that make the problems from our mass communications seem like child's play. We have been living on the edge of a nuclear apocalypse for more than a half-century. More countries are trying to join the nuclear club every year. How long can we have such weapons without using them? If we do not destroy humanity by weapons of mass destruction, we may eliminate our species through biotechnology as we transform ourselves into post-humans. Such biotechnological wizardry was not very long ago the purview of only science fiction writers. Not any more. We are already beginning the process of changing how we are born and when we will die. The gift of children is transforming into a production process where we will be able to select physical and mental qualities. And on the other end of human

1. Richtel, "Growing Up Digital," A 1.

life, there is a search for radical life extension and ultimately eternal life. As we view the current technological horizon, one has to wonder how we will avoid destroying all human life, making ourselves passive recipients of shallow messages and pleasures, or adopting the dangerous eugenic fantasy of transforming our species into transhumans?

In an age confronting such startling possibilities, the monk and spiritual writer, Thomas Merton (1915–1968), is a resource offering an important critique and healing resources for our technology-saturated culture. There were many prompts for his musings on technology. It could be a book given by a friend like *The Technological Society* by the French Protestant theologian, Jacques Ellul. Sometimes, it was a random event. One day he was sitting in the woods on a tree stump and observed a black widow spider and thought he should kill it so that another brother would not sit on the stump and be bitten. He observed that it was odd how human beings in the modern age always expected a technological intervention to solve every problem.

> It is strange to be so very close to something that can kill you, and not be defended by some kind of invention. As if, wherever there was a problem in life, some machine would have to get there before you to negotiate it. As if we could not deal with the serious things of life except through the intermediary of these angels, our inventions. As if life were nothing, death were nothing. As if the whole of reality were in the inventions that stand between us and the world: inventions which have become our world.[2]

After this brief observation, he moved onto another topic. From this example, you can sense both Merton's keen ability for spontaneous reflection and the methodological challenge in writing on Merton and technology. He provided no extended analysis on technology in a single book or article. The closest he came to a systematic analysis were some notes on technology and several tape-recorded lectures on technology to his charges as novice master. Despite these methodological challenges, it is possible to piece together his insights into a coherent and multifaceted analysis of technology. Having outlined his insights in my first chapter, I will then apply this critique to specific technological issues—nuclear weapons, modern communication technologies, and transhumanism.

2. Merton, *Conjectures of a Guilty Bystander*, 24 (hereafter *CGB*).

Acknowledgments

IN PURSUING MY EXAMINATION of Merton and technology, I have relied on a number of resources. All books are collaborative efforts involving many sources and forms of assistance. For my book, there is of course the subject, Thomas Merton, and the writers and ideas that shaped his thinking on the issue of science and technology. The sources for Merton are diverse and would include but not be limited to Jacques Ellul, Leo Szilard, Rachel Carsons, Lewis Mumford, Flannery O'Connor, Pierre Teilhard de Chardon, Neils Bohr, Werner von Heisenberg, and Admiral Hyman Rickover. There are also thoughtful secondary writers who have reflected on Merton and his views of science and technology. These would include the writings of Paul Dekar, Kathleen Deignan, S. N. D., Daniel Horan, O. F. M., Gray Matthews, Paul Pearson, Patrick O'Connell, Dennis Patrick O'Hara, William Shannon, Donald P. St. John, Monica Weiss, and John Wu, Jr. William Shannon's exploration of the categories of "community" and "collectivity" in Merton's writings I have found particularly useful.[3] Likewise, Kathleen Deignan's essay, "The Forest is My Bride," is very important for explaining Merton's reflections in the spiritual aspects of nature.[4] My ideas were greatly assisted by my participation in a conference in 2011 sponsored by the Thomas Merton Center at Bellarmine University titled, "Contemplation in a Technological Era: Merton's Insight for the Twenty-First Century."

In my initial research on Merton, I was blessed with the gracious direction of the theologian, Dr. Larry Cunningham, at the University of Notre Dame who is a preeminent Merton scholar. The International Thomas Merton Society granted me a Shannon fellowship that aided my

3. Shannon, "Christian Living in An Age of Technology," 179–90.
4. Deignan, "The Forest Is My Bride," 21–41.

research. Subsequently, directors of the Merton Center such as Therese Sandock and Paul Pearson have been very helpful. At the Merton Center, I discovered many useful materials, including some revealing letters between the atomic physicist, Leo Szilard, and Thomas Merton. The editors of the *Merton Seasonal* and the *Merton Annual* have published five of my articles on Merton and science and technology. The input of *Merton Annual* and *Merton Seasonal* editors like Victor Kramer has helped to refine my reflections. I have also written a chapter on Merton and technology for my book on the engagement of Catholic intellectuals with science and technology.[5] This book brings together much of my research over the past fifteen years, as well as an array of new material like my analysis of Merton's ideal of wisdom and a chapter on transhumanism.

The last people to assist this project are some gracious readers. On this particular project, I would include John Allard, O. P., a Merton scholar and theologian at Providence College. John's many astute comments have contributed greatly. I have also asked careful readers of Merton like Bud Treanor, Cathy Crosby, Mick J. Elson, and others for their comments. Mary Alma Durrett, the pride of southern Alabama, lent her excellent editing eye to the text. I owe much to my assistant, Beverly Osterbur, for her support and great work. My wife, Beth, and son, William, read and commented on my chapters and they greatly improved the book.

I would like to acknowledge the assistance and permission of the Thomas Merton Center and the Merton Legacy Trust for the use of Thomas Merton's "Technology" and "Lectio Divina" notes in several places in the book. These are notes he prepared for his classes for the young monks at the monastery. Likewise, I would like to thank Lynda Claassen with the Mandeville Special Collections Library of the University of California at San Diego for permission to cite and use a part of a letter from Leo Szilard to Thomas Merton.

Also, I would like to thank Rodney Clapp, my editor at Wipf and Stock, for his hard work, support, and prompt attention to the details of this book.

5. Thompson, *Between Science and Religion*, 111–39.

Introduction

There is no escaping technology . . . It isn't just that we have got a lot of machines. But that the entire life of man is being totally revolutionized by technology. This has to be made very clear. We are not at all living just in an age where we have more tools, more complicated tools, and things are a little more efficient, that kind of thing. It's a totally new kind of society we're living in . . .

Thomas Merton,
"The Christian in a Technological World"

WHEN I WAS A little boy, my grandfather in West Virginia told me that when he was born things were not much different than during the life of Jesus. Okay, Jesus didn't have a railroad or a telegraph, to be sure, but in many respects my grandfather was right. People traveled by horses and read by oil lamps. But our technologies now advance at lightening speeds. For almost a century our computing power has doubled every eighteen months (Moore's Law) and our wireless communications has doubled every thirty months (Cooper's Law).[6]

As a result of such rapid technological advances, we live as Merton stated in a "totally new kind of society" because of technology. Just consider our first hour in the morning after we awake. We are sleeping in homes that are regulated by heaters and air conditioners to provide a comfort zone of temperature. Then the alarm clock rings. We arise to take a bath or shower with internal plumbing that is heated to our preference. We eat a breakfast that has been processed at factories and preserved with chemicals. Even the milk for our cereal comes from a production line of cows who are pumped full of hormones and antibiotics. We sip our coffee

---

6. Ridley, "Why Can't Things Get Better Faster (Or Slower)?".

procured from a machine and watch the morning news on television. Walking outside, we commute to our job in a car, bus, or a subway. We turn on our cell phones. Welcome to your first hour.

These forms of technology seem innocent enough. They make our lives easier, perhaps even more pleasurable, but the advance of technology also presents ethical challenges that are not so benign. Consider these three scenarios.

1) As chapter 2 will discuss, we have developed atomic weapons with the capability to destroy the planet. The containment of such weapons of mass destruction places us in a position of either pursuing questionable attacks based on uncertain intelligence or accepting nuclear proliferation. We wonder how many nations have this weapon. Will we go to war to prevent countries from acquiring a nuclear weapon? But with an increasing proliferation that may eventually extend to terrorists, it is not difficult to imagine that some use of this weapon will result in the deaths of millions at some point.

2) The deluge of data from our modern communications is threatening to overwhelm us in a different way. Consider this one fact—more to follow in chapter 3. It is predicted that we will soon produce five exabytes of digital information every ten minutes. We will produce in roughly an hour the equivalent of all the information in all the books ever written.[7]

3) Our minds and bodies face another threat through the conscious designing of the human species, transforming us into a new technological being, the transhuman. As chapter 4 will suggest, this is no longer science fiction. In a neuroengineering lecture at the Georgia Institute of Technology that I attended by Dr. Michael Chorost on March 9, 2012, he lectured on "How to Put Your Brain on the Internet, Lessons from a Cyborg." He indicated that we are now developing technologies to read and alter our brain activity. He indicated that we will connect our brains through our biotechnologies in the "World Wide Mind."

All of these forms of problematic machinery and techniques are technologies. So before we proceed a fair question to ask is, what is a technology? When I use the term *technology*, I am referring to instruments or processes that control, shape, and modify our environments and to

7. Shermer, "Defying the Doomsayers," A 13.

an increasing degree, in our own time, our selves. These technologies supplement our natural capacities by adding to our physical strength and senses. With the extension of capacities, technologies allow us to manage the natural world in order to meet our needs and desires as a species. With these capacities technologies shape how we live and think.

Thomas Merton's relationship to technologies creating a "totally new kind of society" was ambivalent. He rejected the worse features of a technological world that threatened our humanity, but he knew that we could not ignore technology or revert to a more innocent age. He was amazed at the mastery of technology over nature, but beneath the shiny surface accomplishments of our inventions there lurked inherent problems. Technology was about action, changing nature to conform to our desires. It plunged ahead guided by the imperatives of control, efficiency, and productivity. These imperatives were indifferent to humane concerns about beauty, love, or art. Technologies raised other troubling questions. Could a person be a contemplative in such a world of relentless change? Should we raise important ethical questions? The tension of positive and negative possibilities, for Merton, was never far beneath the surface; they were often expressed in consecutive sentences.

> Yesterday in the morning when I went for a breath of fresh air, before my novice conference, I saw men working on the hillside beyond the sheepbarn. At last the electric line is coming! All day they were working on holes, digging and blasting the rock with small charges, young men in yellow helmets, good, eager hard-working guys with machines. I was glad of them and of American technology pitching in to bring me light as they would for any farmer in the district. It was good to feel part of this, which is not to be despised, but admirable. (Which does not mean that I hold any brief for the excess of useless developments in technology.)[8]

Merton advanced a probing analysis of technology that freely acknowledged this ambivalence. He knew that technology was an unavoidable aspect of modern life even in a monastery. Any monastic calling that ignored technology would turn monasteries into museums. But we needed discernment to determine how technology affirmed or demeaned human life. Merton confided that, "What I am 'against' then is a complacent and naive progressivism which pays no attention to anything but the fact that

8. Merton, *Dancing in the Water of Life*, 206 (hereafter *DWL*).

wonderful things can be done with machinery and with electronics."[9] What was lacking then was the wisdom to know how to accept the undeniable utility of technology without violating the requirements for a fully human life, a life that praises God, aids other people, and nurtures creativity and freedom.

This critique had an interesting trajectory. His views prior to entering Gethsemani in December of 1941 were largely unknown, but there were a few scattered clues. In 1939, under the spell of his latest enthusiasm, James Joyce, he made a list of "modern words" that included "sterile, sterilize . . . Lockheed dive bomber, magnetic mine, heavy and light machine guns, tommy guns, minesweeper . . ." On another occasion after participating in a radio broadcast as a student at Columbia University, he was awed at his instant contact with so many people.[10]

When he entered the monastery in 1941, Merton rejected a modern world infected with corruption and falsity.[11] The former bon vivant of Cambridge University was now a crusading Trappist who contrasted the redemptive mission of the monastery with a fallen America. He later confessed that he entered the monastery with "Thoreau in one pocket, John of the Cross in another, and [was] holding the Bible open at the apocalypse."[12] Even with its relative seclusion in the hills of northern Kentucky, Gethsemani was not immune to secular maladies. The reorganization and expansion of the monastery in the 1940s and 1950s imported a "small-mechanized army of builders" whose noisy machinery built the facilities for a flood of new postulants.[13] He lamented the "infernal concerto of chain saws" with their "yell of hot metal, diabolical intervals of atonal discord."[14]

The problem at the monastery was more than one of external noise. The internal assumptions of a technological mentality had infiltrated the

9. Technically, the abbey is a monastery of the Order of the Cistercians of the Strict Observance (O.C.S.O.). They are known as Trappists because their founding abbey was at Soligny-la Trappe, France. Merton, *The Road to Joy*, 98–99, "Circular Letter" (Lent 1967), hereafter *RJ*.

10. Merton, *Run to the Mountain*, 110, 280, entries of December 14, 1939, December 18, 1940.

11. Merton, *Entering the Silence*, 44, entry of March 11, 1947 (hereafter *ES*); Merton, *DWL*, 225, entry of April 7, 1965.

12. Merton, "Is the World a Problem?," 305.

13. Merton, *Sign of Jonas*, 5.

14. Merton, *CGB*, 308.

cloistered walls. Some monks held that a rigorous adherence to rules and regulations insured salvation. This "pitiful faith" in a mechanical spirituality made Merton's "blood run cold."[15] A psychology of progress had infiltrated the Church at many levels. Merton was astonished that Pope Paul VI referred to contemplatives as "aviators of the spirit." The pope's comments suggested an "illusion" that contemplatives knew the mechanisms guiding the "secrets of interior life" and could use them.[16]

This technical spirituality was allied with another error. The Harvard Business School trained abbot, Dom James Fox, wanted the abbey to be "successful, secure, 'prosperous.'"[17] The monks like cogs in a machine were to efficiently produce their cheese and fruitcake. For Merton this was a mistaken concession to the cultural and economic patterns of the broader society.

With his opening to the world in the mid-1950s, Merton advanced a more nuanced view and admitted that technology, for better or worse, was an inevitable reality for the monastery. Monks in modern air conditioned rooms could no longer claim a separation from technology. He admitted that he treasured a refrigerator and running water when he acquired them at his hermitage at the monastery. Merton adopted a carefully qualified reconciliation not only with technology but also with the persons living in a technological world. A major stimulus in his transformation was the separation of individual persons from the technological and modern systems that had diminished but not eliminated their humanity. As early as August of 1948, during his first visit to Louisville in seven years, he stated that, "Although I feel alienated from everything in the world and all its activity, I did not necessarily feel out of sympathy with the people who were walking around. On the whole they seemed to me more real that they ever had before, and more worth sympathizing with."[18]

Always searching for new insights from an array of sources, Merton would develop, as will be detailed in the first chapter, a prophetic and contemplative critique of technology. He addressed a wide and complex array of issues connected to the technological world. What should we make of materialism, Marxism, capitalism, alienation, technological

15. Merton, *Search for Solitude*, 72 (hereafter *SS*).
16. Merton, *ES*, entry of August 21, 1967.
17. Merton, *SS*, 353, entry of December 6, 1959.
18. Merton, *ES*, 223, entry of August 14, 1948.

warfare, mass society? New issues appeared by the 1960s from questions about DDT, Vietnam, computers, and television.

In analyzing technology, Merton wanted to avoid a further fracturing of the Catholic Church, especially with the advent of the Second Vatican Council. He was not ready to swear allegiance to the opposing camps of traditionalists and progressives. He declared in 1965 that, "I am frankly quite alienated from much of the thinking going on in my Church, on both sides, both conservative and 'progressive.'"[19] This bifurcation of the Church into traditionalists and progressives was problematic because of their foundational assumptions. Merton rejected both "a large mass of passive conventionalists who cling blindly to what is familiar, and a small minority of eccentric faddists who are in love with anything new just because it is new."[20]

Despite being frustrated, Merton wanted to be a "bridge builder for everybody and to keep communication open, especially among fellow Catholics. So much depends on it."[21] The desire to be a bridge builder was the result of a realization that the temptation to quickly judge others was problematic. The faith was "not a kind of radio electric eye which is meant to assess the state of our neighbor's conscience." Instead we should envision faith as a "needle by which we draw the thread of charity through our neighbor's soul and our soul and sew ourselves together in one Christ."[22]

There were other dangers. This binding of humanity in charity must begin with a spiritual connection or it would lose its bearings.

> Those who seek to build a better world without God are those who, trusting in money, power, technology and organization deride the spiritual strength of faith and love and fix all their hopes on a huge monolithic society, having a monopoly over all power all production, and even over the minds of its members. But to alienate the spirit of man by subjecting him to such monstrous indignity is to make injustice and violence inevitable.[23]

---

19. Merton, *Witness to Freedom*, 319, "Letter to Lord Northbourne," (Easter 1965), hereafter *WF*.

20. Merton, *Disputed Questions*, 152 (hereafter *DQ*).

21. Merton, *WF*, 325, "Letter to Rita" (November 14, 1965).

22. Merton, *DQ*, 125.

23. Ibid., 129.

Hence, secular ideologies were not an anchor point for Christians. Moreover, they were transient; the "life expectancy of the average secular ideology today is about five years."[24] He acknowledged that many protests in the world were "little more than pose or declamation."[25] Ideologies with shrill slogans whether communist or capitalist suffered from an inability to ask fundamental questions including a probing of basic premises. Rather than adhere to such ideologies, Merton supported a renewal of culture in Christ. The role of Christian education in this process was to move the technological society beyond its rational and sub-rational levels to engage a transcendent level of experience, the reality that would humanize our lives. In this cultural renewal that was sought by Vatican II, the Church should seek neither domination nor a faddish popularity, neither a rejection of science nor an unqualified adoption of its products—the latest technologies.[26]

For the Church to be successful in this balancing act, its path of wisdom must draw not only on theology, but also on philosophy, literature, and other faith traditions. A full range of human experience must be brought to bear on the subject of technology. This path to wisdom required us to distinguish the "useless or harmful from what is useful and salutary, and in all things glorify God."[27]

In this journey Merton's hard questions and careful reflections addressed the harm resulting from the triumph of technology in the modern world. The problem was not merely the development of new knowledge or capabilities. Indeed, these capabilities were not problematic per se, but they often nurtured a mentality that was destructive of authentic human ends. The technological world and its compulsive mentality were not currently balanced by "other aspects of human existence in the world," and as a result "the very splendor and rapidity of technological development is a factor of disintegration." This was the problem with Marxism that had pushed technological progress to the point of endowing "material things with intellectual life and stultifying human life into a material force." The result of this type of economic and historical reductionism was inevitably "the moral collapse of the material world."[28]

24. Merton, *Faith and Violence*, 148 (hereafter *FV*).

25. Merton, *DQ*, 151.

26. Merton, *CGB*, 13, 53–55, 195; Merton, *WF*, 315, "Letter to Lord Northbourne" (February 23, 1966).

27. Merton, *CGB*, 15.

28. Ibid., 23, 60, 72.

Merton's analysis assumed the need for a careful examination of the problems resulting from a technological mentality dominating culture. My first chapter will initially consider Merton's formulation of the foundations of wisdom in the ideal of purity of heart, theoria physike, and sapientia or wisdom before surveying the specific sources of a technological mentality and its consequences. In analyzing the technological mentality, Merton relied on Jacques Ellul's notion of technique, Lewis Mumford's analysis of urban life, and Hyman Rickover's public policy principles. In the end, as the noted Merton scholar William Shannon observed, Merton sought through such principles the creation of a true community in contrast to a thoughtless technological collectivity.

In the second chapter I will analyze Merton's connecting of modern warfare and a technological mentality as they were applied to atomic weaponry. Turning to the issue of modern communication techniques in chapter 3, I will apply Merton's observations and general insights to assess problems from the current flood of information from constantly evolving communication technologies. Moving from the past and present into the future, chapter 4 will be the most speculative of my efforts and will apply Merton's insights to our ability in the near future to radically alter human nature through a variety of technologies in our search for human perfection. In the end we risk creating another species—transhumans.

In chapters 2–4, the goal is to explore how Merton's search for wisdom can provide a framework for analyzing specific aspects of the technological world. He not only issued prophetic warnings, but as chapter 5 will demonstrate, Merton provided some hope for our troubled culture through careful reflections on humanizing work, applying a measured approach to using technologies, recognizing the role of nature as a source of healing, and the adoption of the philosophy of a solitary.

In all of these chapters, the impetus of the book is to challenge a technological mentality which is seeking to solve problems at hyper-speed and is justified by the mandates of expediency and efficiency. At times, the power of our technological paradigm is startling and even on occasion sublime. Still, we remain uneasy; there are inner yearnings for meaning, love, mystery, and community that remain unfulfilled in our technology saturated world. William Shannon reminds us why Merton's contemplative quest for wisdom and reality is still attractive.

> Those who choose to live a contemplative life are convinced that there is much more to life than what you see. There exists, they would claim, a world of reality below and above (indeed all

around) our ordinary daily experience. It is this world which is alone truly real. People who are content to live simply on life's surface, are completely oblivious to the wonders that exist within them and all about them. How mightily their lives would be changed if they became aware of this other deeper dimension.[29]

29. Shannon, "Can One Be a Contemplative in a Technological Society?," 17.

Abbreviations

CHAPTER I

A Contemplative Critique

In the past the man has been first, in the future the system must be first.

> Frederick Winslow Taylor,
> *The Principles of Scientific Management* (1911)

The intimate connection between technology and alienation is and will remain one of the crucial problems we will need to study and master in our lifetime. Technology . . . bestows the greatest amount of wealth and power upon those who serve it most slavishly at the expense of authentic human interests and values, including their own human and personal integrity.

> Thomas Merton,
> "Answers for Hernan Lavin Cerda"

Contemplative Wisdom

THOMAS MERTON ASKED IN one of his essays, "Can contemplation still find a place in the world of technology and conflict which is ours? Does it belong only to the past?"[1] This is a fair question. After all, Merton conceded that, "our technological society no longer has any place in it for wisdom that seeks truth for its own sake, that seeks the fullness of being."[2] For some of his contemporaries, contemplation was

1. Merton, "The Contemplative Life in the Modern World," 215.
2. Merton, *Choosing to Love the World*, 58.

1

irrelevant in the modern world. Merton was criticized for avoiding an active role on the front lines of issues like civil rights or the Vietnam War. One of his sparring partners on this point, through a series of letters, the theologian Rosemary Radford Reuther, chided him that young monks were leaving the monastery in 1967 because their vocations "would not be expressed in that corner of 'this world' that calls itself 'monastery.'"[3] Merton responded that he was still part of that external world; he was not living in a "sixth century virgin forest with wolves," but amidst farms and managed forests. Moreover, he had neither forfeited his humanity nor his range of interests. Monks were not "hothouse plants, nursed along in a carefully protected and spiritually overheated life of prayer." Rather the contemplative life "implies openness, growth, development." A monk should not be restricted to narrow horizons and esoteric concerns that would "condemn him to spiritual and intellectual sterility."[4]

While the problems of the world were also a problem for a monk, Merton had a broader and less partisan view of current issues since he was not directly engaged in the affairs of the world and was not committed to "particular interests." From his vantage point, he could see the forest and the trees.

> Now its seems to me that if a monk is permitted to be detached from these struggles over particular interests, it is only in order that he may give more thought to the interests of all, to the whole question of the reconciliation of all men with one another in Christ. One is permitted . . . to stand back from parochial and partisan concerns; one can thereby hope to get a better view of the whole problem and mystery of man.[5]

From this broader contemplative perspective, he could more accurately diagnose the problems and develop a prescription of spiritual resources for recovering wisdom in the contemplative tradition. The path towards wisdom began with listening and waiting, "not knowing what is next." And whatever wisdom was for Merton, it was not a simple formula. He declared, "I am not in the market for the ready-made and wholesale

3. Tardiff, ed., "Letter of Rosemary Radford Reuther to Thomas Merton" in *At Home in the World*, 28–29.

4. Merton, *The Hidden Ground of Love*, 506 (hereafter *HGL*); "Letter to Rosemary Radford Reuther" (March 19, 1967).

5. Merton, *FV*, 146.

answers so easily volunteered by the public and I question nothing so much as the viability of public and popular answers, some of those which claim to be most progressive." While he "did not have clear answers to current questions," he did have serious questions and this was the launch point for the search for wisdom.[6]

Probing carefully and avoiding easy answers, Merton crafted a contemplative critique of technology. The first foundation for his critique was to recognize the source and end of our existence. For Merton, man's deepest need was the "direct and pure experience of reality" that was a "living contact with the Infinite source of all being."[7]

The path to connection could take a number of routes. One path was the teachings of the Christian hermits of the fourth century in the Egyptian desert also known as the Desert Fathers and Mothers. They rejected the "shipwreck" of the late Roman world. They decided to no longer "drift along" passively accepting the values of their world. They rejected the false, formal self fabricated by their society and sought their "own true self in Christ."[8]

This path required a fundamental contemplative move, to reject the false self of the ego, the "superficial, transient, self-constructed self." This was done by purging the old self through a life of "solitude and labour, poverty and fasting, charity and prayer." If properly followed, the desert hermit achieved clarity of vision and rest in God. Through this form of "purity of heart," they intuitively became aware of being anchored in God through Christ.[9] In this "purity of heart," they also were tied to others through the "primacy of love." This love was not merely a sentiment or a doing good to others as if they were objects. The identification in love was much deeper; it required a complete inner transformation that produced a deep connection.

> Love . . . means something much more than mere sentiment, much more that token favors and perfunctory alms deeds. Love means an interior and spiritual identification with one's sisters and brothers, so that they are not regarded as an "object" to "which" one "does good." . . . Love takes one's neighbor as one's other self, and loves him or her with all the immense humility and discretion and reserve and reverence without which no one

6. Merton, *CGB*, 6, 173.

7. Merton, "Preface" to Japanese edition of *New Seeds of Contemplation*, 58.

8. Thomas Merton, *The Wisdom of the Desert*, 3–6.

9. Ibid., 6–10.

> can presume to enter into the sanctuary of another's subjectivity. From such love all authoritarian brutality, all exploitation, domineering and condescension must necessarily be absent.[10]

The path to "purity of heart" suggested some of the key features of a contemplative. The key insight from this tradition was the return to a form of simplicity that had been polluted or blocked "by the accumulated mental and spiritual refuse of our technological barbarism." The Desert Fathers reminded us that we could bypass this blockage and return to a very "practical and unassuming wisdom that is at once primitive and timeless."[11]

If the Desert Fathers provided guidance for an internal spiritual quest, there still remained the issue of how we related to nature and salvation history in a technological world. On these issues, Merton relied on the teaching of the great seventh-century Eastern Christian saint, Maximus, on theoria physike (contemplation of nature). At the threshold of the contemplative life, theoria physike allowed the uniting of the hidden wisdom of God with the hidden wisdom in each person. God's communication of this wisdom was communicated through the divine purpose of material reality, the spirit of scripture, and the inner meaning of history revealed through the salvation offered by Jesus. In this wisdom quest, the contemplative united body and soul, sense and spirit, resulting in a "resplendent clarity within man himself." This clarity was a divine gift allowing humanity to pursue creative initiatives in the arts, politics, and spirituality.[12]

We could veer from the enlightened path of theoria physike through our granting primacy to our senses that precluded our connecting to the presence of spiritual realities in nature because this path was under the control of our egos. We were tempted to adopt a crude and selfish utility in order to manipulate the natural world. In this approach, technology sought "the impersonal, pragmatic, quantitative, exploitation and manipulation of things." From the narrow lens of technology, the ultimate logos or higher purpose of these objects was, as we used to say in law, irrelevant and immaterial. This was a key error of the modern world; it removed the divine from the realm of nature. For Merton, part of the insight of the French Jesuit Pierre Teilhard de Chardin's evolutionary theology was

10. Ibid., 17–18.

11. Ibid., 11–13.

12. Merton, *An Introduction to Christian Mysticism*, 121–26.

that it offered a sense of the divine operating in nature but did so without sacrificing "scientific objectivity or technological utility."[13]

The need for a purity of heart and the insights of theoria physike were aspects of the ultimate quest for sapientia (wisdom). This wisdom detected the source of reality that is beyond purity of heart, theoria physike, reason, or even intuition. This "hidden wholeness" was the source of the pattern and order of the cosmos. Any engagement with this reality must employ but also transcend our rational and intuitive faculties.

> Sapientia is the Latin word for "wisdom." And wisdom in the classic as well as Biblical tradition is something quite definite. It is the highest level of cognition. It goes beyond scientia, which is systematic knowledge, beyond intellectus, which is intuitive understanding. It has deeper penetration and wider range than either of these. It embraces the entire scope of man's life and all its meaning. It grasps the ultimate truths to which science and intuition only point . . . Wisdom is not only speculative, but also practical: that is to say it is "lived."[14]

By seeking this "hidden wholeness" as a "lived experience," we could begin to discern the pattern and order of the universe that is the work of Christ as Logos or creator. Merton thought of this form of wisdom as Sophia, who renewed creation through her love. Sophia was communicated to Merton by a "wordless gentleness" that flowed from the "unseen roots of all created being." In these communications she displayed the virtues of tenderness and mercy and exhibited the qualities of spontaneity, joy, and freedom.[15]

There were spiritual temptations in the search for wisdom. For example, Merton rejected a faith that privileged in its teachings the letter of the law and the resulting cases, distinctions, and decisions. On the other end of the spiritual spectrum, some were suggesting the path of hallucinogenic drugs to achieve spiritual enlightenment. For Merton, the desire to chemically manipulate a mystery typified the worst tendencies of a technological mentality. True mystical experiences were divine gifts, not experiences for purchase. Each person must be open to the gift of spiritual possibilities present in every day.[16]

13. Ibid., 127–31.

14. Merton, *The Literary Essays*, 98–99.

15. Merton, "Hagia Sophia," 363; for an extensive explanation of Merton's use of Sophia, see Pramuk, *Sophia*.

16. Merton, *HGL*, 436–39, "Letter to Aldous Huxley" (November 27, 1958).

The rational and objective processes of Western science that veri-
fied truths through experimentation and empirical verification did not
acknowledge this search for spiritual contact at the center of human
meaning. In pursuing wisdom Merton did not deny the truths of science
or the utility of technology. But science had lost its "wisdom" and "cosmic
perspective" in order to "gain power and promote technical know-how."[17]
The result: humanity was doomed to a path of manic activism and futility.

> We would like to be quiet, but our restlessness will not allow
> it. Hence we believe that for us there can be no peace except
> in a life filled up with movement and activity, with speech,
> news, communication, recreation, and distraction. We seek the
> meaning of our life in activity for its own sake, activity without
> objective, efficacy without fruit, scientism, the cult of unlimited
> power, the service of the machine as an end in itself.[18]

Why did we choose this path? The fundamental error of modern man
and the source of our restlessness was a Promethean desire for control of
our own destiny. We sought to steal the fire of the gods and for what ends?
We did it because like Prometheus modern man was "guilty, rebellious,
frustrated, unsure of himself . . . alienated, yet seeking to assert himself."[19]
We were isolated in our nothingness and yet we rebelled, yearning to
make our own meaning, our own way, to transcend ourselves by our own
powers instead of finding ourselves in God through the charity and self-
lessness of Jesus Christ.

In this Promethean quest, we mistakenly privileged *"external means
to external ends."* Our egos thought happiness could be found in external objectives like power, control, popularity, fame, or physical beauty.
We employed external means like wealth, plastic surgery, hallucinogenic
drugs, machines, and status symbols to achieve these external ends. This
quest was selfish and aggressive. It offered no hope of balance or peace
because there was no answer, no technique that would satisfy such false
desires.[20]

Once we rejected the claims of the technological world and began
the pursuit of wisdom, we must avoid some additional blind alleys. We
would be tempted to veer from a worship of the world to a denial of

17. Merton, *WF*, 71, "Letter to Rachel Carson" (January 12, 1963).
18. Merton, "Contemplative Life in the Modern World," 216.
19. Merton, *The New Man*, 23–33.
20. Merton, "Contemplative Life in the Modern World," 217.

the world. Our goal should not be a life of abstraction that excluded the world through an act of will and sought a specious isolation in a spiritual ghetto. Rather, we should live in the world and "plunge into the very midst of contradiction, by the acceptance of emptiness and suffering, by the renunciation of the passions and obsessions with which the world is on fire." The contemplative remained cool in the heart of this "fire" by engaging the world while he abandoned the false idols of the self.[21] The path of contemplative wisdom thus presented a vision that was challenging and complicated, but was open to anyone with an "instinct for truth" and a desire to be free from a servitude to "external things." We must separate from the world, our false self, and our external quest for control in order to be spiritually reintegrated. As a reintegrated being, we could connect to others who complete and fulfill our beings in a spirit of giving and love.[22] At its core contemplative wisdom sought the path to reality that was not only "a way of good works and of loving devotion, good as these are, but also a way of emptiness and transcendence in union with the crucified Christ."[23]

A Contemplative Analysis

The aforementioned basic principles of "Sophianic" wisdom prepared Merton to engage in a sustained analysis of the complex issues confronting a technological society. These principles would not be easily applied to a chaotic and disorienting technological world. In this context Merton warned that,

> It is precisely this illusion, that mechanical progress means human improvement, which alienates us from our own being and our own reality. It is precisely because we are convinced that our life, as such, is better if we have a better car, a better TV set, better toothpaste, etc., that we condemn and destroy our own reality and the reality of our natural resources. Technology was made for man, not man for technology. In losing touch with being and thus with God, we have fallen into a senseless idolatry of production and consumption for their own sakes . . .We no

---

21. Ibid., 218.

22. Merton, *The Inner Experience*, 21–22.

23. Merton, "Contemplative Life in the Modern World," 223.

longer know how to live, and because we cannot accept life in its
reality life ceases to be a joy and becomes an affliction.[24]

Technologies had too often ceased to be about aiding humanity
but had become about the demands of the machine. This problem was
evident in the monastery where machinery replaced human effort. The
result was too often "a deadening of spirit and of sensibility, a bluntness of
perception, a loss of awareness, a lowering of tone, a general fatigue and
lassitude, a proneness to unrest and guilt . . ."[25]

Beyond the monastery, Merton sensed a technological mindset with
a dangerous compulsion to control nature and its processes. This was an
ancient fallacy reflected in Adam's prideful act of trying to improve his
"wisdom and science" in the Garden of Eden. In Eden, humanity exchanged a "perfectly ordered nature elevated by the highest gifts of mystical grace for the compulsions and anxieties and weaknesses of a will left
to itself . . ."[26] This idolatry violated key tenets of contemplative wisdom
by prompting a "withdrawal of love from God, in order to love something
else . . . If we idolized something limited, we withdrew our hearts entirely
from the service of the living God."[27]

Already leery of the impact of technology on a fallen human nature,
Merton's reading of the works of the philosopher of science and technology, Lewis Mumford, and the theologian, Jacques Ellul, provided additional theoretical ballast for his critique. Mumford reminded him that
the technological revolution narrowed the possibilities for human flourishing. The dominant cultural question had become, "will this work?"
instead of "what is it?" or "is it right?" Consumed by a naive devotion to
progress, a heedless culture pursued its blind lunge into the future.[28]

In the fall of 1964, Merton received a copy of Jacques Ellul's *The
Technological Society*. Ellul was in some ways a curious source for inspiration. He was, according to the theologian Martin Marty, "the quint-
essential Protestant"; quick to criticize Catholics for the lack of biblical
grounding in concepts like the natural law and was often labeled as too

24. Merton, *CGB*, 222.

25. Ibid., 25.

26. Merton, *The New Man*, 110–11.

27. Merton, *The Courage for Truth*, 277, "Letter to Henry Miller" (August 7, 1962),
hereafter *CT*; Merton, *No Man Is an Island*, 18.

28. Thomas Merton, *DQ*, 178–79; Merton, "The Christian in a Technological
World."

pessimistic about technology.[29] Nonetheless, Merton, as recorded in his journal, was thrilled to have discovered such an ally.

> Reading Jacques Ellul's book, *The Technological Society*. Great, full of firecrackers. A fine provocative book and one that really makes sense. Good to read while the Council [Vatican II] is busy with Schema 13 (as it is). One cannot see what is involved in the question of "The Church in the Modern World" without reading a book like this. I wonder if the fathers are aware of all the implications of the technological society? Those who resist it may be wrong, but those who go along with all its intemperances are hardly right.[30]

From his monastery in Kentucky, Merton wrote about Ellul's insights to Bernard Haring, who served during 1962 to 1965 as secretary of the commission that drafted at the Second Vatican Council the Pastoral Constitution on the Church in the Modern World, *Gaudium et Spes*. Ellul's works needed to be discussed at Vatican II, because the Council must account for what Ellul termed "technique," a mentality of progress and change that trapped humanity in an "automatic self-determining system in which individual choices had largely ceased to count."[31] Systems of warfare, work, and consumption sought only the ends of efficiency, productivity, and progress. Ethical or spiritual considerations were marginalized or ignored. Instead, technique relied on the myth that each person was an autonomous creature capable of constant improvements leading to a liberation of the human condition. Paradoxically, the result of technique was alienation not freedom for those seeking autonomy, because "technology alienates those who depend on it and live by it. It deadened their human qualities and their moral perceptiveness. Gradually, everything becomes centered on the most efficient use of machines and techniques of production, and the style of life, the culture, the tempo and the manner of existence responds more and more to the needs of the technological process itself."[32]

---

29. Marty, "Creative Misuses of Jacques Ellul," 4.

30. Merton, *DWL*, 159–60, entry of October 30, 1964.

31. Merton, *HGL*, 383–84, "Letter to Bernard Haring" (December 26, 1964). Merton was introduced to Jacques Ellul and Lewis Mumford through Wilbur Ferry at The Center for Democratic Institutions. Ferry had arranged a translation of Ellul's work. Shannon, "Can One be a Contemplative in a Technological Society?," 13.

32. Merton, "Answers for Hernan Lavin Cerda," 3–12.

Merton realized that the totalizing claims of "technique" opposed any religion that was not fully attuned to the requirements of efficiency and progress. Instead, the all encompassing demands of technique guided political and social life towards a mass society because of a "vast uncontrolled power that is leading man where he does not want to go in spite of himself . . ."[33] In a culture guided by "technique," propaganda, and advertising, slogans became the preferred communication forms, adapted to the need for speed and simplicity of a technological society. In contrast to the use of religious symbols that point to a greater reality, Merton observed that advertising presented a commodity in its "crudest, rawest, and most violently appetizing form" that we must buy, consume, use, and replace. The seductive formulation of advertisers suggested emotionally pleasurable alternatives to religion.[34] Moreover, advertisements and propaganda replaced any "systematic ethical speculation" and the need to "reason out, calmly and objectively, the moral implications of technical developments which were already superseded by the time one knows enough to reason about them."[35] A pacified citizenry did not accept the challenge of discovering within themselves the "spiritual power and integrity which could be called forth only by love."[36]

The mentality of "technique" spread by propaganda inevitably infected social values. The market orientations of contemporary society presumed that human beings were "biological machines endowed with certain urges that require fulfillment."[37] Each person thus became a commodity designed to meet the demands of others. The goal in our romantic relationships was to be a worthy product or to negotiate a profitable deal. Merton concluded that, "We unconsciously think of ourselves as objects for sale on the market. We want to be wanted. We want to attract customers. We want to look like the kind of product that makes money. Hence, we waste a great deal of time modeling ourselves on the images presented to us by an affluent marketing society."[38]

The problem with this market approach was that love, properly understood, was about giving; it was about sacrifice. It was not a market

---

33. Merton, *HGL*, 383–84, "Letter to Bernard Haring" (December 26, 1964).

34. Merton, *DQ*, 272.

35. Merton, *CGB*, 65.

36. Merton, *DQ*, 133–34.

37. Merton, *Love and Living*, 29 (hereafter *LL*).

38. Ibid., 29.

exchange. Love was thus a form of worship which responded to "the full richness, the variety, the fecundity of living experience itself: it 'knows' the inner mystery of life."[39] The individuals participating in this mystery were transformed into a new entity through a conversion to love in their souls.

Why would a society accept a regime of "technique" that threatened our spiritual vitality? It was the consequence of a bargain that exchanged moral and spiritual integrity for the lure of unprecedented power. Once again, humanity erred by pursuing external means to external ends. This bargain was akin to the temptations of Christ in the desert to pursue power and control.[40] The modern world offered new technical forms of these ancient temptations. Merton noted that the physicist, Max Born, concluded that technology was often a triumph of the intellect instead of reason. The intellect distinguished between the possible and the impossible, while reason distinguished between the sensible and the senseless. Applying Born's distinction, Merton concluded that manned space flight was a triumph of the intellect and a failure of reason.[41]

A society guided solely by intellect would not have the resources to constrain technology. Merton affirmed with Jacques Ellul that "technique" would control humanity through technocrats, as in the case of manned space flight, who determined our needs on the basis of the requirements of their systems. These systems became autonomous as reasoning persons were gradually eliminated. There was no compromise with this agenda and the citizenry must "take it or leave it." Most Americans did not opt out of the technological society because the prosperity resulting from the productivity was assumed to be "signs of election," a divine blessing.[42]

Pacifying us with the seductions of slick advertising, wealth, and the possibilities of unprecedented powers, technology had the authority to massively alter the psyche of the human species. There was the very real possibility of a serious "depersonalization of man in mass-technological society."[43] Technology had increased and improved the range of

39. Ibid., 34.
40. Merton, *The New Man*, 23–29.
41. Merton, "Answers for Hernan Lavin Cerda," 6–7.
42. "Technology," 54; Merton, *SS*, 234, entry of December 7, 1958.
43. Merton, "Technology," 55.

consumer options and control of nature, but at the sacrifice of individual creativity and integrity.

Seeking Allies

In engaging technology Merton rarely commented extensively on the views of other Catholic writers. He knew that Catholic thinkers were at both ends of the spectrum on technology. The theologian Jean Danielou acknowledged that, "Nothing is more Biblical than technology" and the theologian Ernst Benz's *Evolution and Christian Hope* tried to transform the Bible into a treatise in favor of technological innovation. Other Catholic scholars, like the sociologist Louis Massignon, feared the notion that God's creation required a perfecting by technology.[44]

Merton turned to other resources for developing his ideas. He recognized that writers of fiction provided a valuable witness to the problems of a technological mentality. He appreciated Flannery O' Connor's novel, *The Violent Bear it Away*, in which the myth of the expert was expressed through a schoolteacher who was "illuminated and blessed with a scientific world view" and was "acquainted with all the best methods for helping people become happy and well-adjusted in the best of all possible societies." The teacher was determined to liberate a young boy from the "obscurantism and superstition" of one of his family members, "the prophet." The teacher was the apostle of technique and "this is precisely what his [the teacher's] *hubris* consists in: the conviction that the infinite rightness and leveling power of 'scientific method' has given him a mandate to transform other people into his own image: which is the image of nothing. And though he is 'nothing,' yet others, he knows it well, belong to him, since he has science on his side."[45] O'Connor thus provided a valuable criticism of the "infallible process of reducing everyone to the same void." The technological man inhabited this void full of "boredom, emptiness, neurosis, psychoanalytic illnesses, etc." Responding to this malaise, O'Connor presented the case for "personal and spiritual liberty against determinism and curtailment."[46]

44. Merton, "Technology," 54; Merton, *WF*, 319, "Letter to Lord Northburne" (June 4, 1967).

45. Thomas Merton, *Mystics and Zen Masters*, 258–62.

46. Ibid.

In formulating his critique, Merton also scanned contemporary intellectual life for allies beyond the Catholic world. He observed that despite the advent of totalitarian political regimes and the adoption of "technique" in every dimension of human life, there were glimmers of hope for a common front. For example, there was a widespread intellectual rebellion against science and technology.[47]

> This protest is articulated by artists and writers who have developed an eschatology of their own, sometimes clear-sighted in its analysis, generally anarchic and negative in its view of the future. It is a poetic protest of those who claim to speak for man against a completely mechanical and dehumanized world-view, a fake humanism which is easily judged by its fruits—cold war, political and economic pharisaism, the total irrationality of mass-society . . .[48]

Merton applied the term "vitalism" to this form of cultural protest that encompassed such diverse sources as Sigmund Freud and the existentialists. Vitalism did not reject technology per se but did reject its totalizing tendency that denied the human dignity of each person. A Catholic would not share theological ground with such writers, who were often atheists and agnostics, but there was common ground to be explored in vitalism's rejection of the "objectivity of science" and in its recognition of the "primacy of the living subject." The individual was a nexus of spontaneity, uniqueness, self-expression, and fulfillment, but this focus on the individual tended in vitalism to excessive emotion and exaggeration. This exploration could double back on itself and resent the demands of "spirit." As a result, there was an "anti-humanist" aspect in vitalism that glorified irrational and subconscious forces. This dimension was often exhibited in times of conflict and could result in resentment and even nihilism.[49]

What about other religious or philosophical traditions? Much of Eastern religious and philosophical wisdom was helpful in its insistence on denying the control of the material world. A particularly useful antidote to Western materialism was Zen Buddhism, which taught Merton that we must recognize that which is in our life without our efforts.[50]

---

47. Merton, *WF*, 293, "Letter to Leslie Dewart" (June 28, 1963).

48. Merton, "The Church and the 'Godless World-4,'" 3.

49. Ibid., 3–9.

50. Padovano, *The Human Journey*, 123.

Many Eastern thinkers realized that humanity was mistaken in trying to control such external realities, like nature. One of the best descriptions of the futility of human control was the poem, "The Inner Law" of the Taoist philosopher Chuang Tzu, as translated by Merton.

> He who is controlled by objects
> Loses possession of his inner self:
> If he no longer values himself,
> How can he value others?
> If he no longer values others,
> He is abandoned.
> He has nothing left![51]

In rejecting the false claims of the external material world, the wisdom of the East recovered an "immediate awareness" of the spiritual life that had not been dimmed by "technical progress." The traditional religions of the world understood the wisdom of a withdrawal into our interior self in order to face the "deepest forces of reality itself." It was only in this interior quest that there could be a true recovery of the fullness of the soul.[52]

Collectivity or Community

In Merton's application of contemplative wisdom, there was no easy formula, no algorithm. Contemplation was "a kind of spiritual vision to which reason and faith aspire, by their very nature, because without it they must always remain incomplete." While we could cooperate in this process, the ultimate knowledge of God in our lives was a gift of the Holy Spirit. This gift was a concrete manifestation, a living presence and not the pursuit of abstract truths. The objective was an "awakening, enlightenment and the amazing intuitive grasp by which love gains certitude of God's creative and dynamic intervention in our lives." Grounded in this form of divine contact, the relationship of the contemplative to other selves was premised on an analogous recognition of the true relationship of God and each individual. The individual was not created to be an isolated autonomous unit, a consumer, or a cog in the machinery of a technological mentality. Rather, each person was destined for a life of

---

51. Thomas Merton, *The Way of Chuang Tzu*, 136–37.

52. Merton, *The Asian Journals of Thomas Merton*, 157. Merton is relying in this passage on the work of Conze, *Buddhist Thought in India*, 81.

dialogue with God and one another that thrived in "the soil of freedom, spontaneity, and love."[53]

The maintenance of such soil required the nurturing of authentic Christian communities and the avoidance of the lure of the false collectivity of the technological society. In true communities the fulfillment of the individual person and the progress of society were inextricably linked.

> The transformation of society begins within the person. It begins with the maturing and opening out of personal freedom in relation to other freedoms—in relation to the rest of society. The Christian "giving" that is required of us is a full and intelligent participation in the life of our world, not only on a basis of natural law but also in the communion and reconciliation of interpersonal love. This means a capacity to be open to others as persons, to desire for others all that we know to be needful for ourselves, all that is required for the full growth and even the temporal happiness of a fully personal existence.[54]

Technology had a role in this community and was welcome insofar as it could "provide means for the expression of Christian love, and prepare the way for the unity of the human family in peace and reconciliation."[55] More specifically, the technological advances of the modern world, properly oriented, could assist humanity with a decent standard of living and sufficient time for reflection.

For Merton, modern life in a technological society lived under the shadow, however, of a collective mentality that offered pleasure, wealth, and power. The technologically driven collectivity was united by the desire to preserve the "enormous," "obsessive," and "uncontrollable fabrications" of our "false selves." Individuals, under the illusion that they were autonomous beings, abdicated "conscience, personal decision, choice and responsibility." In the "freest" of societies, we meekly accepted our collective illusions. Why? A collective ignorance and passive acceptance of advertising and slogans was the "axiomatic foundation of all knowledge in the human collectivity." Technology aided this seduction into a mind numbing passivity by providing an ever-increasing material abundance that justified the demands of the collectivity.[56]

53. Thomas Merton, *New Seeds of Contemplation*, 1, 5, 14, 21.

54. Merton, "The Church and the 'Godless World-1,'" 5–9.

55. Ibid., 8–9.

56. Merton, *Thoughts in Solitude*, xi.

How then to resist the siren call of the collective society? Merton noted that there were two alternative paths to the claims of collectivity that were not mutually exclusive. The individual could choose social activism and opt to assist others, "without thought of personal interest or return."[57] We could seek to raise our brother or sister out of servitude and "squalor, whether physical or spiritual" through social structures that affirmed freedom, friendship, love, and creativity. The danger in such efforts was that the frenzy of the activist could destroy their capacity for inner peace and would "kill the root of inner wisdom which makes their work fruitful."[58]

Another option that was not mutually exclusive with a life of social justice was adopting a contemplative life that confronted and accepted poverty, renunciation, and death. This approach challenged the illusions of the collectivity, promoted peace and understanding, and cultivated honest relationships.[59] This contemplative path sought a wisdom wherein life was seen in its wholeness with stability and purpose.[60]

A fully human life could only be achieved in a community where individuals had "faces, identities and histories of their own" and could communicate with one another in the "openness and dialogue of love." In contrast to the advertising slogans and propaganda of the collectivity, a community accepted the reality that the human communication of one's self was in "confrontation with and in free, vital relation with the existence and potentialities of the other." Each person in the community had a freedom that was "a liberation from control by what is less than man or entirely exterior to man."[61]

Having presented the alternatives of collectivity and community, Merton summarized our alternatives.

> What we have then is a conflict between two concepts of community: a false and arbitrary fiction, a collectivist togetherness, in which all possibility of authentic personal existence is surrendered and one remains content with one's neutral quasi-objectified presence in the public mass; or a genuine community of persons who have first of all accepted their own fragile lot, who have chosen to exist contingently and thereby have accepted the

57. Merton, *Raids on the Unspeakable*, 14–16, hereafter *RU*.

58. Merton, *CGB*, 81–86.

59. Merton, *RU*, 17–23.

60. Merton, *CGB*, 83.

61. Merton, "The Other Side of Despair," 217–37.

solitude of the person who must think and decide for himself without the warm support of collective fictions.[62]

In order to more clearly state the differences, here is a list of the alternative sets of principles of collectivity or community. They can be listed as follows:

Collectivity	Community
1. Favors material progress and prosperity;	1. Favors the priority of moral growth and the dignity of the human being;
2. Grants a priority to the pursuit of exotic and scientific achievement instead of human values;	2. Grants a priority to the knowledge of the community and each person as a member of the community;
3. Promotes an excessive focus on work, internally generated goals and timetables in an obsession to reach higher levels of production;	3. Promotes a humanizing conception of work that should not be boring, routine or monotonous, but in harmony with human creativity and dignity;
4. Supports unassisted human reason to discern and achieve proper ends;	4. Supports both spiritual and rational forms of knowledge;
5. Promotes technologies that dull human intelligence through the cultivation of passive technologies;	5. Promotes technologies that sharpen the intellect;
6. Divides individuals who accept what has been forced on them by social manipulation.	6. Nurtures an integration of each person of body, mind and soul through what has been freely accepted.

Merton's principles of community provided useful general criteria and objectives, but how do we make choices in specific complex situations? Such decisions required coherent rules and procedures to nurture the creation of community. One rule was that technology could best "serve man" within a nuanced rule of law that facilitated balanced judgments. Another key assumption was that scientists and engineers were not necessarily the best individuals to evaluate the legal and ethical parameters of their actions because they focused on efficiency not morality and often had a vested financial interest in such decisions.[63]

Having posited the guidance of a rule of law that was not encumbered by excessive self-interest, how do we develop the criteria for enacting specific laws or making critical decisions? To respond to this need,

62. Ibid., 226.
63. Merton, "Technology," 55–56.

Merton provided his novices principles from Admiral Hyman Rickover's lecture, "A Humanistic Technology." In 1964 Rickover, the father of the nuclear Navy, proposed a set of sensible public policy guidelines that could be used to solicit answers that were consistent with the general principles of a true community.

1) The short-range private goals of all interested parties must be balanced with a consideration of the common good,

2) The health and lives of citizens must be protected and even extended to insure the "psychic health" and the ineffable nature of every human person,

3) Any technology must conform to the principle that the liberty of an individual ends where it harms another,

4) A technology must be assessed in advance as to its potential for harm. The technology should not be applied until it can be rendered harmless,

5) Authorities should consult and listen carefully to the advice of their experts.[64]

These criteria when rooted in the deeper vision of the principles of contemplative wisdom and a true community offered a sound basis for making deliberate and thoughtful choices that provided a means to guide public policy.

The Path of Prophetic Resistance and Contemplative Wisdom

In the course of this chapter, I have presented key principles guiding Merton's contemplative critique. At the core of this search for wisdom was adherence to "God's transcendent and secret holiness." This contemplative quest was not done alone, however, but was a joint practice of a Christian community, a place that privileged human dignity and a balanced life of work and spiritual enrichment. This community also employed a variety of spiritual resources, including art and liturgy, to draw its members closer to the transcendent ground of our being. A

64. Merton, "Technology," 55–57. Merton's notes are based on Rickover, "A Humanistic Technology," 3–8. This article is from Admiral Rickover's speech that he gave at Georgetown University's Symposium on Cybernetics and Society in November of 1964.

failure to pursue this path would have important consequences because in the absence of contemplation, "we remain small, limited, divided, partial; we adhere to the insufficient, permanently united to our narrow interests, losing sight of justice and charity, seized by the passions of the moments, and, finally, we betray Christ. Without contemplation, without the intimate secret pursuit of truth through love, our action loses itself in the world and becomes dangerous."[65] In contrast, a contemplative wisdom was rooted in a theology that appealed to "the deepest moral idealism of a civilized tradition"; it sought allies in other faith traditions, and fostered a constructive dialogue with secular humanism based on the latter's "need for wisdom." It developed communities that nurtured the full range of human flourishing instead of a mindless submission in collective systems.[66]

In his promotion of a contemplative wisdom, Merton's views were not always popular. Who appointed this Trappist monk in Kentucky to be a cultural watchdog? How could he justify his role? Merton answered these questions by observing that any denial of "the anguish of being a true prophet" meant that we had chosen "the carrion comfort of acceptance in a society of the deluded by becoming a false prophet and participating in their delusions."[67] While a martyr suffered physical death, a prophet suffered an "inspiration or vision" of the judgments and truths of God. A prophet bowed in fidelity to divine imperatives.[68]

In his prophetic role, Merton knew that the criticism of a monk must be forthright and fearless, but it must also be nuanced and prudent. The proper course was located between the opposing poles of a rejection of and a submission to the technological world. Thus, he commended the Vatican Council for moving from "a radically negative anti-science and anti-technology attitude to something more open and humane." Nonetheless, Christians must contribute to the development of a critique that developed a proper understanding of technologies that reversed or redressed the false mandates of "technique."[69]

Guided by Merton's critique of technology, the subsequent chapters will address specific problems related to technology, some of which were

65. Cunningham, *Thomas Merton and the Monastic Vocation*, 209.

66. Merton, *Mystics and Zen Masters*, 114–15.

67. Merton, *FV*, 68.

68. Merton, *DQ*, 222–23.

69. Merton, *DWL*, 324, entry of December 13, 1965; Thomas Merton, *LL*, 48–69.

critical in his lifetime and in ours and some of which are more peculiar to the contemporary world or the future. In either case, his insights can guide us to a more humane world. There is much that depends on these efforts. Merton warned that, "without wisdom, without the intuition and freedom that enable man to return to the root of his being," technology would promote a life of "compact and uncompromising isolation."[70]

70. Merton, "Preface" to the Japanese Edition of *Seeds of Contemplation*, 60.

CHAPTER 2

Avoiding the Nuclear Apocalypse

Mr. President, I'm not saying we wouldn't get our hair mussed,
but I do say no more than 10 to 20 million killed—tops!

> General Buck Turgidson describing for the President the "mi-
> nor" casualties from a nuclear war in the movie,
> *Dr. Strangelove* (1964)

It is frightening to realize that . . . "Christian society" is more
purely and simply a materialistic neo-paganism with a Christian
veneer. And where the Christian veneer has been stripped off,
we see laid bare the awful vacuity of the mass-mind, without
morality, without identity, without compassion, without sense,
and rapidly reverting to tribalism and superstition. Here, spiritual religion has yielded to the tribal-totalitarian war dance and
to the idolatrous worship of the machine.

> Thomas Merton,
> *Peace in the Post-Christian Era*

A Casualty of War

IN THE SUMMER OF 1942, Thomas Merton's only brother, John Paul,
was training to be part of a bomber crew in Canada. On a leave,
John Paul visited his brother at the monastery. Both stood in unfa-
miliar clothing, one in the habit of a Trappist monk and the other in
the uniform of a sergeant in the Royal Canadian Air Force. John Paul

wanted to become a Catholic. After some preparation, he was baptized and received into the Church with both brothers receiving communion together. It was the last time they would see each other. On April 16, 1943, John Paul's bomber had a malfunction and crashed in the English Channel. His back was broken on impact and he was placed in a raft where he cried in torment for water. He died and was buried at sea. Thomas Merton had lost his mother at 6, his father at 16, and now his only brother at 28.[1] This death inspired a poem, "For My Brother: Reported Missing in Action, 1943."

> Where and in what desolate and smokey country
> Lies your body, lost and dead?
> And in what landscape of disaster
> Has your unhappy spirit lost its road? . . .
> When all the men of war are shot
> And flags have fallen into dust,
> Your cross and mine shall tell men still
> Christ died on each, for both of us.[2]

An Urgent Problem

The agony of war was now personal. For the remainder of his life, the issue of war remained a central concern of Thomas Merton. He was not naive about the response his comments might evoke. Merton admitted, "that this whole unpleasant issue of war is a delicate one to handle. I know too that people are very upset and excitable, and that it is very difficult to keep a straight perspective when discussing such a critical problem. It is very unfortunate that many people think that the mere fact of hesitating to approve an all out nuclear war makes a man by that very fact a communist."[3]

By the 1960s, Merton declared that war was the most urgent problem of modern man. In 1962, he predicted a major war by 1967. To counter this possibility, he declared that Christians were under a divine imperative to disarm and live in peace and "this is the one great

---

1. Mott, *The Seven Mountains of Thomas Merton*, 221–22.

2. Merton, "For My Brother: Reported Missing in Action, 1943" in *The Collected Poems of Thomas Merton*, 36.

3. Merton, *WF*, 32–33, "Letter to J. F. S" (February, 1962).

lesson that we have to learn. Everything else is trivial . . ."[4] The pervasive violence in the world offended his deep longing for peace, balance, and a humane world. A failure to deal with armed conflict threatened any kind of spiritual progress and the formation of humane communities. The project of the Second Vatican Council to promote a viable Christian humanism was impossible amidst the ceaseless devotion to the creation and use of military power.[5]

Some hint of these concerns about warfare came early. He prepared a notice of conscientious objection in the spring of 1941. While he accepted the Catholic just war doctrine, he could not see "killing people with flamethrowers as any form of Christian perfection."[6] In his famous autobiography, *Seven Story Mountain* (1948), the young monk recorded his disgust with the century of "poison gas and atomic bombs." The United States was on the "doorsill of the apocalypse."[7] The presence of military posts near Gethsemani was a source of enervation. In 1947 the guns at Fort Knox were "tuning up for war."[8] Two years later, Merton admitted that the constant artillery practice near the monastery had evoked a "feeling of uneasiness in the pit of my stomach" for over seven years. His opposition to atomic weaponry was unequivocal by 1951.[9] A more solid theoretical framework in the 1960s strengthened these early concerns. By then he concluded that the march to mass destruction through a nuclear war was a result of the mentality of technique that prompted ceaseless military improvisation. The war machine was speeding "downhill without brakes."[10]

The rapid explosion of new military technologies preoccupied both the communists and the Western democracies. Merton labeled the ideological camps, per the battling entities in the books of Ezekiel and Revelation, Gog and Magog. Merton fully recognized the terrible human rights violations of communist regimes including the persecution of religions. The communist ideology was more rigid and monolithic, but he acknowledged some similarities between communism and capitalism

---

4. Merton, *CGB*, 214–19.

5. Merton, *FV*, 259–87.

6. Merton, *RJ*, 10, "Letter to Mark Van Doren" (Lent, 1941).

7. Merton, *Seven Story Mountain*, 94.

8. Merton, *Sign of Jonas*, 81.

9. Merton, *ES*, 452, entry of March 3, 1951.

10. Merton, *Peace in the Post-Christian Era*, 103–04, hereafter *PCE*.

in their idolization of material realities and adopting of a mentality of technique. Based on these false premises, Gog (the communists) desired power and Magog (the capitalists) desired wealth. These shallow goals left both of them spiritually barren. They were opportunistic and pragmatic, blindly passive in their submission to a "demonic activism."[11]

Despite their shallowness and futility, each ideology demanded devotion to its "cause" that was justified by a "state of mind." A "state of mind" was a foundational set of perceptions that was composed of a number of "superficial assumptions" about the world and its processes. The present "state of mind" of both Gog and Magog grounded in a pervasive materialism bred a mutual "truculence and suspicion." Suspicion of the other justified increasingly destructive technologies because of "the needs of the moment."[12]

The "state of mind" was powerful because of its claim to being objective. Each side imagined that their causes and only their causes were "fair, objective, practical and humane." Taking their objectivity for granted, they did not carefully probe and check the facts of their side, their cause. Indeed, we manipulated the facts to fit our worldview. Merton concluded that, "objectivity becomes simple dogmatism."[13] This dogmatism threatened to spark a global collapse into another war, perhaps the last war. There were powerful forces that benefited from the plunge into darkness. The machinery of war undergirded national affluence. It was a new product line and Merton commented, "An H-Bomb I am told costs only two hundred and fifty thousand dollars to make. Was there ever such a bargain? I ask you, who can give you more destruction for your dollar? Is it believable that we can resist getting all that we have paid for?"[14]

Because of the absolute requirements of the contemporary "state of mind," nations were free to create military technologies that threatened to eliminate entire societies. These weapons were not the brain children of evil scientists but the result of a moral callousness in the fabric of a technological society that placed a priority on efficiency and progress. Such goals lacked rationality. Clichés about liberty, faith, and an adherence to

11. Merton, "Letter to Pablo Antonio Cuadra," 372–91.

12. Ibid.

13. Merton, *FV*, 154–55.

14. Merton, *CGB*, 218.

material prosperity disguised an essential emptiness.[15] The embracing of this emptiness by political elites spread a "motiveless violence."[16]

This "motiveless violence" was demonstrated in the Vietnam conflict and was personified in President Lyndon Johnson's Secretary of Defense, Robert McNamara, who was trained at Ford and directed the mass production of death in a remote country. McNamara embodied the modern bureaucrat who had "incredible technical skill and no sense of human realities." He was lost in "abstractions, sentimentalities, myths, delusions." More broadly, the war was the product of "good ordinary people" whose "surface idealism" and "celebration of warm human values" hid their allegiance to a technological regime of expansive capacities and swift progress. Ellul's "technique" advances the folly of the United States in Vietnam and "comes from the blind obsession with mechanical efficiency to the exclusion of all else: the determination to make the war machine work, whether the results are useful or not." Military systems in this context were prone to uncontrollable paroxysms of destruction producing a "sick feeling that the big machine has gone on the rampage again and no one can really control it." Increasing violence and destruction in Vietnam only provoked higher levels of resistance.[17]

While he wrote extensively about the Vietnam War, the problem of nuclear war was the deepest concern for Merton. There was the constant reminder of this possibility in the airplanes of the Strategic Air Command flying over the abbey. These planes were described in various journals as "technological swans," "ponderous sharks," and "apocalyptic cherubs." They were "enormous, perfect, ominous, grey, full of Hiroshimas."[18] The people on the ground were just numbers to these planes. Each person was merely a unit in a calculus of destruction.

Could the values of the modern nation state prevent a nuclear cataclysm? Merton doubted it because of our devotion to military technology. He observed in the poem, "Original Child Bomb," that the *Indianapolis*,

15. Merton, "The Church and the 'Godless World-3,'" 3–7.

16. Merton, *HGL*, 161, "Letter to James Douglas" (November 6, 1965).

17. Merton, "Answers for Hernan Lavin Cerda," 5–9; Merton, *WF*, 109, "Letter to Père Herve Chaigne" (April 21, 1965); Merton, *LL*, 41, 109–10, entries of April 16, 1966 and June 6, 1967; Merton, *FV*, 109–10.

18. Merton, "Day of A Stranger" in *Spiritual Master*, 215. Merton's certainty that the planes belonged to the SAC command may be dubious, but the presence of military aircraft is certain. Merton, *DWL*, 72, 131, 169, 190, entries of February 7, 1964; July 28, 1964; November 24, 1964; and January 9, 1965.

a cruiser carrying the radiation for the bomb to Tinian Island in World War II, had instructions that if the ship was sinking to save the nuclear fuel before any human life. The nuclear weapon had become an end in itself, an idol. Moreover, language was distorted on behalf of the atomic project. Merton recalled the allied code names on the mission that employed terms from birth, motherhood, and religion. Churchill was cabled after the first successful Los Alamos test that "babies satisfactorily born." The scientists called it "little boy" and placed it in the "womb" of a B-29 named after the pilot's mother. The original atomic bomb was code named "Trinity" as it would bring a new beatitude, a vision of ultimate destruction instead of eternal life. After delivering the bomb, the plane headed for the "Papacy."[19]

The spare verses of "Original Child Bomb" slowly released the measured fury of the poem. Here was a vivid depiction of the unreality of an act that was too calm, logical, and detached. The tone of detachment signaled that the danger of nuclear war was not from insane men obeying insane orders, but from sane men following sane orders. The defense expert, Herman Kahn, in *Fortune* magazine declared "reasonable" an entire set of options that would result in the killing of millions.[20] The proposed use of nuclear weapons was "cool and deliberate," based on the calculations of a computer employing ladders of escalation.[21]

The nuclear systems and strategies of the superpowers could thus arrive at a paradox, a nuclear war without anyone wanting it because if they did X, we must do Y. Complex realities and considerations must not be reduced to such an equation. In contrast to ideological slogans, there must be a careful reasoning process instead of the "fake technical objectivity of the engineers of death, who talk of the extermination of millions as if it were a matter of killing flies."[22] As for naive idealists, Merton chided those who wished to merely concentrate on the horror of weapons of mass destruction. Their energies should be redirected at controlling such powers. He found some merit, for example, in the plan of the physicist and "father" of the hydrogen bomb, Edmund Teller, for a

19. Merton, *Original Child Bomb*, 293–302.
20. Merton, *DWL*, 245–46, entry of May 1, 1965.
21. Merton, *CGB*, 209.
22. Merton, *CT*, 126, "Letter to Ernesto Cardenal" (September 11, 1961).

limited and purely defensive tactical nuclear strategy as a means to prevent an unlimited conflict.[23]

Merton's analysis was foundational as well as strategic; he was also
seeking the social, psychological, and economic causes of war. The modern technological war was a new type of conflict that hid its collective
virulence unlike acts of individual violence.

> Modern technological mass murder is not directly visible, like
> individual murder. It is abstract, corporate, businesslike, cool,
> free of guilt-feelings, and therefore a thousand times more dead-
> ly and effective than the eruption of violence out of individual
> hate . . . But our antiquated theology . . . blesses and canonizes
> the antiseptic violence of corporately organized murder because
> it is respectable, efficient, clean, and above all profitable.[24]

This respectable, efficient, clean, and profitable warfare annihilated scores
of innocent victims. Merton had met with some Hibakusha who were
the Japanese victims of the American atomic bombs and he knew that
the abstraction of nuclear war might end in the death of many similarly
innocent people.[25] The disjunction of technological success and human
annihilation in atomic weapons was possible because there was an insufficient grounding in non-technical values, particularly transcendent
ones. Human beings, in the rush to production and progress, became a
product, a thing to be manipulated and perfected or if necessary deleted.[26]

Merton penned a poem, "Chant to Be Used in a Procession Around
a Site With Furnaces," that described the extreme objectification of human life in the engineering of the Nazi concentration camps. Merton had
read some of the memos of the engineers and commandants at the concentration camps and he used many of their phrases in the poem.[27] The
object of the engineer/narrator was to efficiently produce a more perfect
society as the machinery of death improved "upon human weakness"
and produced "soap." The end of the poem about Auschwitz reminded
the contemporary Western world that they too harbored a technological
mentality and a comparable incapacity for self-examination. A warning

23. Merton, *Turning Toward the World*, 218, entry of May 10, 1962 (hereafter, *TTW*).

24. Merton, *FV*, 7.

25. Merton, *DWL*, 104, entry of May 17, 1964.

26. Merton, *SS*, 299, entry of June 30, 1959; Merton, *TTW*, 4, entry of May 25, 1960.

27. Merton, *CGB*, 241.

at the end of the poem proclaimed, "Do not think yourself better because you burn up friends and enemies with long-range missiles without ever seeing what you have done."[28]

In November of 1964, there was a retreat at Gethsemani with noted peace movement activists like Philip and Daniel Berrigan and John Yoder. The issue of technology became a central focus of this gathering. The discussions centered on whether a technological society was inherently oriented to self-destruction or could be redeemed in a new "sacral order."[29]

This "sacral order" was the Kingdom of God, a path beyond Marxism and capitalism and the false collectivities of the modern world. The goal was not the freedom of the Soviet Man after the mythical "withering away of the state," nor the chaotic irresponsibility that leaves Western man the captive of economic, social, and psychological forces "[but] the freedom of the Sons of God, on earth, in which individual life becomes the life story of God and its contents filled the vast expanses of the universe."[30]

This "new sacral order" would be difficult to achieve and required an "*inner renewal of the Christian and of his Church*." In this renewal the Christian conscience must not remain a "vestigial faculty." The Christian conscience must rediscover an internal spiritual communion with the "hidden ground of our being." This "hidden ground" was revealed in the "human compassion and charity of Christ." From this grounding in reality, the Christian could recover a moral orientation and reach correct judgments.[31]

> One must have profound and solid grounding in spiritual principles, one must have a deep and persevering moral strength, a compassion, an attachment to truth and humanity, a faith in God, an uncompromising fidelity to God's law of love. Failing this, a nebulous and all pervading 'state of mind' will take the role of morality and conscience, and will rationalize its prejudices with convenient religious or ethical formulas. The result will be a fatal turning away from truth and from justice.[32]

28. Merton, "Chant to Be Used in a Procession Around a Site With Furnaces" in Merton, *Collected Poems*, 345–49.

29. Merton, *The Nonviolent Alternative*, 259–60.

30. Merton, *DQ*, 24.

31. Merton, *PCE*, 124–162.

32. Ibid., 91–92.

The Christian must carefully apply this approach to modern nuclear warfare. Dangerous simplifications resided within either the complete resignation of the pacifist or the indifference to carnage of the foreign policy realist and his drive to preserve the national interest. The situation required a subtler analysis. Extraordinary technological advances must also prompt a reconsideration of the validity of Catholic just war theory because of the risks to humanity. In the place of just war, realism, and traditional pacifism, there was another possibility for evaluating war, the ideal of "relative pacifism." Relative pacifism occupied a moral no man's land, a territory of contradictions and tensions. It assumed that nuclear war would "almost inevitably" violate all the conditions of a just war. Hence, peace negotiations through international organizations must be sought without capitulation or escalation.[33]

The Scientist and Nuclear War

As noted in chapter 1, Merton's notes for a lecture to his novices on technology cited with approval some public policy principles of the founder of the nuclear navy, Hyman Rickover. One of the admiral's essential principles was that political authorities should listen to their technical experts. Merton observed that scientists like Neils Bohr, Leo Szilard, and Werner Heisenberg were among those who eventually grasped the problems with their atomic discoveries in a "widely human way." Their caution could be contrasted with the proponents of a "narrow scientism" whose horizon considered only the short-term technical consequences of their actions.[34]

Why had many scientists, albeit a bit tardy, exhibited sensitivity to the ethical dimensions of the nuclear project? In a chapter on nuclear scientists in *Peace in the Post-Christian Era*, Merton declared that a divinely inspired moral or natural law written on the heart of each person insured such an outcome.

> The natural law has not been and cannot be abrogated. It is written in the hearts of all men, including Communists. It can of course be violated and silenced and indeed it is frequently and systematically violated, and has been for centuries in numberless ways both by societies and individuals. Still it must be recognized that the voice of conscience cannot be permanently

33. Merton, *PCE*, 83.
34. Merton, *LL*, 244, entry of June 3, 1967.

silenced. Men will continually be confronted with truth. Even if
natural ethics do not guarantee protection against the danger of
nuclear war, there should be at least a vestige of sanity and common sense that would make us all realize that massive nuclear
destruction should be avoided . . .[35]

In a somewhat curious move, Merton was prone to give scientists the
ethical benefit of the doubt even if they had ignored the natural law. He
readily exonerated atomic scientists for not being able to stop their weapons from being deployed by political leaders. The physicist, Neils Bohr,
could not be blamed for working on the atomic bomb project because he
was a "modest soft spoken man, a reflective man and not an operator."[36]
Albert Einstein was a "great prophet of the now dead age of liberalism.
He emerged with the disconcerting kindness and innocence of the lib-
eral, came forth from the confusions of his day to produce for us all a
little moment of clarity, and also, as an afterthought, he left us the atomic
bomb. But we cannot take the bomb as a pretext for looking down on his
liberalism, or doubting his benevolence."[37]

And why did Merton give Einstein and other scientists a pass on
an ethical condemnation? Scientists on the Manhattan project did not
express a moment of hesitation about the atomic bomb after the Nazi
surrender and the threat of an atomic weapon by an Axis Power was removed. Perhaps the scientists should have developed their consciences
and their moral sensibilities earlier. Were good intentions or detachment
a sufficient excuse for their actions? Was Merton sufficiently aware of
the dangers of an ethic of intention instead of an ethic of responsibility?
Shouldn't we have a moral duty to anticipate certain outcomes from our
actions?

In defense of Merton's analysis, it is worth remembering that many
scientists had morally awakened after the Second World War and by the
time of Merton's comments, they were agitating against nuclear weapons. Unlike the politicians, they confronted their mistakes and willingly
reversed their positions. The *Bulletin of Atomic Scientists* was advancing
a disarmament agenda. The politicians, however, listened to the minority of scientists like Edward Teller and Herman Kahn, who told them
what they wanted to hear. In fairness, Teller and Kahn wished to avoid

35. Merton, *PCE*, 110.
36. Merton, *LL*, 245, entry of June 6, 1967.
37. Merton, *CGB*, 99.

the use of nuclear weapons, but they supported the acceleration of the development of nuclear weapons under the assumptions of mutually assured destruction. The danger was that this acceleration invited a nuclear apocalypse.[38]

Merton developed a correspondence with one of the scientists opposing this acceleration, Leo Szilard. This physicist provided a rare "civilized voice" in the age of the nuclear arms race. In the early 1960s Szilard had contacted the monk about his proposal for a peace lobby. Merton acknowledged that these proposals were "as close as anything I have seen fitting on with Catholic moral teachings and the Popes."[39] Specifically, Szilard held that one of the superpowers must make the first move, and he recommended a limited unilateral initiative. The United States must adopt a defensive strategy that did not aim at the massive destruction of civilian populations. The United States would openly declare that it would not bomb Russian cities and army bases with atomic bombs unless the Russians first initiated such an attack. Moreover, a warning to civilian populations would precede any detonation of atomic bombs. Tactical nuclear weapons would only be deployed for defensive measures.[40]

Merton was impressed by these ideas. He wondered whether it was possible to bring Szilard and the other peace movement leaders under a common umbrella organization in order to exert some collective pressure on the political process. To secure a common effort, he wrote Szilard a letter in April of 1962 praising the scientist's recent initiatives and offered to donate royalties from a recent book to a Catholic peace group. The letter criticized certain Catholic proponents of nuclear weapons while praising scientific opposition to the bomb that countered the "absurd, inhuman, and utterly distorted assumptions that have become the basis of thinking of the majority."[41] Szilard responded that he was grateful for the interest and promised to keep Merton notified of his program for securing signatures in opposition to nuclear weapons. When Szilard died two years later, there had been no additional contacts. The opportunity for

---

38. Merton, *PCE*, 112–122. Merton did not lump all proponents of nuclear war into one basket. Kahn and Teller were distinguished. Teller, in contrast to Kahn, ruled out a preemptive strike or massive retaliation except as a final expedient.

39. Merton, *WF*, 55, "Letter to Father J. Whitney Evans" (June 13, 1962).

40. Merton, *PCE*, 119–120.

41. Merton, *WF*, 38, "Letter to Leo Szilard" (April, 1962).

close cooperation was lost, perhaps because of the extent of their other commitments and the late date of their communications.[42]

Inconvenient Warnings

Merton's ideas on war and military technologies were suspect in the Church and the broader American society. His articles constantly warned of the dangers of a nuclear war between October of 1961 and October of 1962. Merton's protests prompted warnings and then an order from Abbot General Dom Gabriel Sortais to not publish any more articles on issues of war and peace. Merton was entering the realm of public policy controversy and bringing unwanted attention to the monastery. The Abbot General reminded him that the order was devoted to prayer, not teaching, but there were some precedents in Merton's favor. Bernard of Clairvaux, the founder of the Trappists, had offered advice to those in power. There was another problem. Merton was attacking the long-standing Catholic position of just war. Despite such concerns, Merton published two articles under pen names. He also had articles that were eventually titled, "The Cold War Letters," mimeographed and circulated among friends.[43]

Despite the censoring of his ideas, Merton believed that the Church could be a vehicle for the promotion of peace. He took solace from John XXIII's positions in the encyclical, *Pacem in Terris*, which approved many of the pacifist themes that were being censored in Kentucky. The encyclical condemned the arms race as a threat to human dignity and pleaded for peace on the basis of "a humaneness, a reason, a compassion which both the 'world' and the Church are capable of understanding."[44] This plea included a call for the restraining of nuclear weaponry. Merton slyly noted to the Abbot General that it was a good thing that the pontiff was not a Trappist monk for he would have been in trouble. The Abbot General countered that the encyclical did not change the restrictions on his writing about nuclear war. John XXIII had written only about aggressive war, not self-defense. The problem with Dom Sortais' distinction is that his just war categories of aggression and self-defense had become less

42. Szilard, "Letter to Thomas Merton."

43. Shannon, "The Year of the 'Cold War Letters,'" 166–171; Merton, "Foreword" to *Saint Bernard of Clairvaux*, v-viii.

44. Merton, *CGB*, 317.

applicable because of the speed and destructiveness of nuclear weaponry. Moreover, the creation of such weapons removed the notions of restraint and proportionality in waging war that were keystones of traditional Catholic just war theory.[45]

While it is hard not to have some sympathy for Merton's position, I have a concern. Once they existed nuclear weapons were very difficult to eliminate, because of the level of technical issues in monitoring their reduction and elimination. The evidence of recent decades suggests that we still do not have foolproof means for accurately monitoring the nuclear capabilities of other countries. We invaded Iraq thinking we would find weapons of mass destruction and there were none. There is also the real possibility of a mistake or miscalculation. During the Cuban missile crisis an unarmed ICBM launch was not canceled, bringing the world perilously close to a nuclear holocaust.[46]

Moreover, nuclear weapons had, in admittedly a very unsettling way, maintained a standoff between the United States and the Soviet Union which created a Cold War but prevented in all likelihood a third world war. I was in a class at the University of Georgia Law School in the 1980s on international law that was taught by the former Secretary of State Dean Rusk. He had discussed in one class the possibility after World War II of an international agreement eliminating nuclear weapons. I approached Secretary Rusk after the class and asked if the elimination of such weapons might have meant a third world war. He acknowledged that such a war might well have resulted from a nuclear ban, but at least it would have eliminated the possibility of a future nuclear war. His view sets a very steep price for the elimination of nuclear weapons. Was it worth risking millions dying in a conventional war? Time may justify his answer, but it has not done so to this point since we have avoided both a nuclear war and a conventional third world war.

Still, the concerns of Rusk and Merton about the insanity of destroying the human race through a deliberate policy of mutually assured destruction remain worthy of very careful consideration. Indeed, major foreign policy cold war warriors like Henry Kissinger, George Schultz, Sam Nunn, and William Perry have formed a loose coalition for eliminating nuclear weapons. This "partnership" realizes that we live on a razor's edge.[47] A wager that superpowers will not opt for mutual nuclear

45. Mott, *The Seven Mountains of Thomas Merton*, 386; Merton, *PCE*, 68–69, 80.
46. Sagan, *The Limits of Safety*, 78–80.
47. Taubman, *The Partnership*.

annihilation is indeed a wager that has the ending of sentient life on the planet as one possible outcome. Such an outcome is hardly imaginable, much less acceptable. For Merton, the American public and politicians had become too comfortable with the possibility of this total destruction. This acceptance of nuclear warfare was the result of "almost total passivity and irresponsibility on the moral level, plus demonic activism in social, political and military life."[48]

This state of affairs regarding nuclear weapons was a direct denial of our humanity, of our vocations as children of God. It assigned our fate to mindless forces of technology, progress, and nationalism. Process trumped principle in this context. The slide to ethical acceptance of mass destruction was illustrated in World War II where permitted targets for the Allies went from being restricted to only military facilities to entire cities. For Merton wars in the modern technological context unleashed "a massive suspension of conscience" in which the only requirement was "destroying the enemy."[49] A potential result of this instrumental form of analysis was violence and destruction on an unimaginable scale. In the face of such horror, Merton urged the restoration of our moral conscience on issues of warfare. Ultimately, he argued that we must align ourselves with life and creation or be subjugated to systems and technologies of destruction.

48. Merton, *PCE*, 104.
49. Merton, *CGB*, 228.

Chapter 3

Reforming the Information Age

The greatest need of our time is to clean out the enormous mass of mental and emotional rubbish that clutters our minds and makes of all political and social life a mass illness . . . The purification must begin with the mass media. How?

Thomas Merton, *Conjectures of a Guilty Bystander*

Is There a Problem?

IN AN AFFLUENT SUBURB of San Francisco, Kord Campbell goes to sleep with a laptop or iPhone on his chest, and when he wakes, he goes online.[1] Nearby, he has a workstation with two computer screens gushing with new e-mails, blog postings, and online chats. Kord's obsession with information technology has consequences. Major problems have arisen because he escapes into video games during times of emotional stress. He forgets things like family dinners. On family vacations, he has trouble separating from his array of devices. He has one child whose grades are seemingly suffering from being online too much. His eight-year old daughter claims he favors technology over the family. His wife struggles with his addiction but accepts that, "He loves

---

1. Apparently, Kord is not alone. Sixty-four percent of American adults, according to a recent Pew Foundation survey, have slept with their cell phones on next to or in their beds. Lenhart, *Cell Phones and American Adults*, 11.

it. Technology is part of the fabric of who he is. If I hated technology, I'd be hating him."[2]

Technology is part of who he is? I know this is figurative speech, but isn't it a bit scary? On the other hand, am I so different? When my iPhone buzzes, I jump to discover who is contacting me. There is a mental compulsion to be connected. I would label this stress as "compulsive communication anxiety." It illustrates how communication technologies can overwhelm our consciousness through an unceasing info-glut that may limit our most important interactions with family and friends. And what happens to faith in such a world?

Thomas Merton lived in an age when the modern communications revolution was just beginning. To be sure, he had grown up with radio, but technologies with much greater capacities such as televisions and computers had limited capacities and use compared to our own age. Nonetheless, his contemplative principles provide prescient insights relevant to our age.

As I discussed in the first chapter, Merton declared that a Christian had a duty to recognize and critique technologies that dehumanized our world. Laboring under the "truth and the judgments of God," Christians must exercise a prophetic role in assuming a "critical attitude toward the world and its structures." Although sternly prophetic at times, Merton's slashing criticisms of technology were often mixed with bemused observations. In *Cables to the Ace*, he ponders how to write a prayer to a computer. "Write a prayer to a computer? But first of all you have to find out how It thinks. Does It dig prayer? More important still, does It dig me, and father, mother, etc., etc.? How does one begin: 'O Thou great unalarmed and humorless electric sense . . .'? Start out wrong and you give instant offense. You may find yourself shipped off to the camps in a freight car. Prayer is a virtue. But don't begin with the wrong number."[3]

The idea of a computer as a living entity is no longer as odd as it would have been in the 1960s. There is talk now of a CASA (computers as social actors) reality. Clifford Nass, who directs a laboratory at Stanford University that studies CASA, has discovered that we respond differently to male and female computer voices and we will be more honest in

---

2. Richtel, "Attached to Technology and Paying a Price."

3. Merton, *Cables to the Ace*, 5–6.

evaluating problems with a computer if we are on a neutral machine and not our own. He wonders if we are afraid of our computer's reaction.[4]

Taking this a step further, you can now get an iPhone application that lets you interact and select the "perfect" virtual girlfriend. Apparently, through a variety of dialogues and activities, you can "romance one of over one hundred polygon partners." Depending on your answers and choices, you can earn a score of up to twenty. A score of twenty means success; you are perfectly matched with a nonexistent, non-embodied, non-sentient polygon partner.[5] Congratulations.

The Communications Tsunami

Before applying Merton's approach, I will sketch the current predicament—its sources and consequences. The first point regarding our predicament is that we have experienced an explosion of communication technologies since Merton's passing in 1968. Consider the following lists of communication devices in existence as of 1968 and 2010.

1968	2010		
Telephone	Cell phone	Laptop computers	Facebook
Telegraph	Internet	Powerpoint	Fax
Television	TV-cable/satellite	iPod	Twitter
Radio	CD/DVD	E-mail	iPad
Record player	Personal computer	Skype	

Not only are there more devices but each new technology reaches a majority of the population much faster. It took sixty-seven years for the telephone to reach 75 percent of the American population.[6] The number of Internet users in the developed world went from 2.4 citizens per one hundred in 1994 to 58.6 per one hundred by 2006.[7] The number of world-wide Internet users passed two billion in 2011.[8] This includes one billion Facebook users."[9] It is predicted that we will download 36 billion

4. Nass, *The Man Who Lied to His Laptop*.
5. Black Dog i-Tech Series, *iPhone & iPad: The Essentials*, 57.
6. Putnam, *Bowling Alone*, 247.
7. Steve Metz, "Editor's Corner."
8. "Internet Usage Statistics."
9. Fowler, "Facebook: One Billion and Counting."

apps in 2012 and 136 billion apps by 2017.[10] The number of hours on the Internet is also rapidly increasing. North American Internet usage, for all persons, was 15.3 hours per week in 2008.[11] The number of text messages increased 160 percent in one year from 2007–2008.[12] The average American teen now sends a mind-boggling 3,000 texts a month.[13] Users of electronic devices ages 8 to 18 spend on average of seven and a half hours on electronic devices per day.[14] Has the ascension of the computer and smart phone meant the decline of the television? Surprisingly, average hours of television viewing by Americans increased two percent between 2008 and 2009, to 153 hours a month.[15] So where are we? In summation, a majority of people in the United States spent at least eight and a half hours a day looking at a television, computer monitor, or a telephone screen.[16] These statistics on Internet and television viewing lead to an important conclusion: looking at a screen is our most common activity.

With the advent of the digital self, screen technology is rapidly replacing the previous print culture of books, newspapers, and journals as our primary form of communication. Less than 6 percent of adult Americans read more than one book a year and 50 percent of young adults (18–24) do no pleasure reading at all.[17] Daily newspaper readership in the United States has declined from 67 percent in 1965 to 43 percent by 2010. The pace of the decline is getting faster. In a stunning development, daily newspaper readership declined 10.6 percent for the period April 2009 to November 2009 compared to the same months in 2008.[18] Young adults between the ages of twenty-five and thirty-four read printed materials for just forty-nine minutes a week in 2008, which was a decline of 23 percent from 2004.[19] Given these declines, particularly among younger adults, the print culture appears to be headed for oblivion over the next couple of generations.

10. "The Best Way to Do Almost Anything on Your Mobile Devices," R 1.

11. Aboujaoude, *Virtually You*, 19–22.

12. Reardon, "U.S Text Usage Hits Record Despite Price Increases."

13. Turkle, *Alone Together*, xiv; Hafner, "Texting May Be Taking a Toll on Teenagers."

14. Lewin, "If Your Kids Are Awake They're Probably Online."

15. Boehret, "Using Another Screen to Interact with the TV."

16. Carr, *The Shallows*, 86–87.

17. Berman, *The Twilight of American Culture*, 26.

18. Ahrens, "The Accelerating Decline of Newspapers."

19. Bureau of Labor Statistics, "American Time Use Survey," 5.

Is this loss of print sources really a problem? After all, there are quite a few positive aspects to these technologies. Taking my own denomination as an example, Catholics can now go online to research saints, popes, encyclicals, spirituality, social justice, and much more. The U. S. Catholic Conference has 29,000 Facebook fans and its own YouTube channel. Pope Benedict XVI has now tweeted.[20]

Our communication devices also provide the means to instantly communicate worthwhile information and projects to other human beings around the world. There are wonderful instances of charity and human connection because of these technologies. Consider how new communication technologies are assisting Do Something, a non-profit to get teenagers involved in helping others. Do Something used social media to get teenagers involved in a successful effort to gather and sent two million books to post-Katrina New Orleans.[21] In addition, people who are homebound now have many new outlets for human interaction. Democracy movements have used communication technologies to coordinate their efforts.[22] In addition, communication technologies allow unprecedented scope and speed of access for the retrieval of data. There may be another benefit. We can eliminate the elitist values of the print world.[23] We are all publishers. The screen has stormed the communication barricades for us. There is a democratization of texts in terms of sources and readers from new information technologies. Power to the people?

Yet, for all the real or imagined benefits of the new technologies, the evidence of serious negative impacts remains troubling. Paradoxically, in an age of instant connectivity, there is a greater isolation of individuals and a pattern of unhealthy social development. The new capacities to shape our communications allows everyone to create new identities in our own self-defined worlds. Even in his lifetime, Merton observed this phenomenon and declared that modern life nurtured the belief that every person could act like a "little autonomous god, seeing and judging everything in relation to [ourselves]."[24] As the political scientist Robert Putnam explored in *Bowling Alone*, participation in the community and

20. Martin, "Status Update," 13–16.

21. Strom, "Charities Go Mobile in Appeal to Young," B 1, 4.

22. The extent of the value of new communication technologies for democracy and democratic movements is hotly debated. Cf. Kalathil and Boas, *Open Networks, Closed Regimes*; Hindman, *The Myth of Digital Democracy*; Shirky, *Here Comes Everybody*.

23. Carr, *The Shallows*, 111.

24. Merton, *CGB*, 294–95.

civic life of the United States has been declining and the media torrent, while not the sole cause, has contributed to the precipitous decline of our common life. Putnam in 2000 wanted a pledge from his fellow citizens to *"find ways to insure by 2010 that Americans will spend less leisure time sitting passively alone in front of glowing screens and more time in active connection with our fellow citizens. Let us foster new forms of electronic entertainment and communication that reinforce community engagement rather than forestalling it."*[25] His request has been largely ignored.

There are of course those who claim that there has been the creation of communities online with those of common interests. There are role-playing games that bring us together for interaction, but these acts of community provide a limited basis for human connection.[26] Research suggests that these communities are occasions for self-fulfillment instead of solidarity. Moreover, these online communities have allowed themselves to be turned into commodities, niche markets for commercial interests.[27]

There is another issue with online communities. The director of the Obsessive Compulsive Disorder Clinic at the Stanford University Medical Center, Dr. Elias Aboujaoude, in his book, *Virtually You: The Dangerous Powers of the E-Personality*, details the impact of the development of "e-personalities" from our online lives. There are some positive aspects. An "e-personality" can allow us to "transcend debilitating shyness, let go of stultifying ambitions, and forge connections and friendships that would be impossible otherwise." But his research also suggests how online communities encourage troubling personality disorders like a loss of inhibitions and an increase in acting out more frequently than in real life. Many "e-personalities" are also subject to increasing delusions of grandeur.[28]

Even more troubling is that these behaviors over time begin to seep into many of these users' offline worlds. According to Dr. Aboujaoude, our digital self can negatively impact our real selves when there are no traditional checks from culture or religion. There is a high propensity for stimulating aggression from easy access to screen violence. And why not? Ninety percent of games for ages eight to eighteen contain violence. One study by the Center for Violence at Iowa State University indicates

25. Putnam, *Bowling Alone*, 410.

26. See Ling, *New Tech, New Ties*; Rosen, "Everyone is Talking"; Castranova, *Synthetic Worlds*; Putnam, *Bowling Alone*, 216–46.

27. Song, *Virtual Communities, Bowling Alone Online Together*, 87–99.

28. Aboujaoude, *Virtually You*, 20–42.

that students exposed to violence at the beginning of the school year were twice as likely to show aggressive tendencies later in the school year.[29] In the virtual realm there is anonymity, a loss of inhibitions, and a greater propensity for aggression. Ryan Brunn was charged with raping and killing a 7 year-old girl in his apartment complex in Canton, Georgia in December of 2011. According to several reports, the young 22 year-old man was uniformly polite with no police record. His on-line personality was quite different, exhibiting large doses of foul language and swagger.[30]

Other mental health problems among the communications generation have continued to increase. To be sure, these problems have multiple sources. Nonetheless, they seem to thrive in the new screen age. The use of psychotropic drugs in the United States by adolescent children rose by 60 percent from 1994–2001.[31] Eight million adolescent children were on psychotropic drugs by 2009.[32] It is estimated that the number of children and adolescents with mental health issues leading to significant functional impairment is now 11 percent.[33] Suicide is now the third highest cause of death for persons 15–24.[34]

What kind of culture is emerging? In its worst features, we are building a culture with increasing mental instability. Less disturbing but still unhealthy is a shallowness built on the demands of passing fads invading our senses through relentless streams of sounds and images. The sociologist, Todd Gitlin, in his book, *Media Unlimited: How the Torrent of Images and Sounds Overwhelms Our World*, summarizes the cultural impact of the communications revolution.

> The most important thing about the communications we live among is not that they deceive (which they do); or that they broadcast a limited ideology (which they do); or that they emphasize sex and violence (which they do); or that they convey diminished images of the good, the true, and the normal (which they do); or that they corrode the quality of art (which they also do); or that they reduce language (which they surely do)—but with all their lies, skews, and shallow pleasures they saturate our

29. Aboujaoude, *Virtually You*, 102–4.

30. Stevens, Leslie, and Scott, "Mom Urges Execution," A1, A18.

31. Zito, et al., "Psychotropic Patterns for Youth," 17–25.

32. Morris and Stone, "Children and Psychotropic Medication."

33. Glied and Cuellar, "Trends And Issues In Child And Adolescent Mental Health Care," 39–50.

34. American Academy of Child and Adolescent Psychiatry, *Facts for Families*, 10.

> way of life . . . streaming out of screens large and small, or bub-
> bling in the background of life, but always coursing onwards.
> To an unprecedented degree, the torrent of images, songs, and
> stories has become our familiar world.[35]

But perhaps there is a pedagogical silver lining. There are champions of the new social media who suggest that creativity and imagination are being prompted in novel and amazing ways by the new technologies. The problem is that our educational systems are not properly measuring the new forms of learning. We are learning as much; it is just in a different form. Our brains are being rewired to capture the rich diversity and multiple possibilities in every context.[36]

The problem is that there is little to no social or biological science to support such claims. In contrast, we know that books and articles challenge readers to think slowly and deepen the analytical and judgment features of the brain. Contemporary studies of young people reading books demonstrate that as they read more they develop specialized brain areas that can rapidly decipher texts. Freed from the problem of slowly decoding texts, they can then build a capacity for "deep reading" that makes them more contemplative, reflective, and creative.[37]

But the protest is raised yet again: you are merely objecting to what is new. Stop being such a curmudgeon. After all, complaints have always appeared with the creation of a new communications technology. In ancient Greece, Plato complained in the *Phaedrus*, through his characters, Socrates and Phaedrus, of the negative experience of the written word that did not allow the probing insights of a live dialogue.[38]

Fair enough. But a case can be made that the new communication technologies are on balance detrimental to our cognitive capacities. The impact of this communications revolution is different. Both screen and print sources provide us texts, but we read very differently when we scroll and click. When a reader scrolls and clicks, they move very rapidly between texts and images rarely pausing very long on any one text or

35. Gitlin, *Media Unlimited*, 6. The impact of the changing forms of communication has been detailed in the last half century by a variety of prophetic voices. See McLuhan, *Understanding Media*; Postman, *Amusing Ourselves to Death*. De Zengotita, *Mediated*.

36. Davidson, *Now You See It*. In a refutation of her science, see the neuroscientist, Changizi, "Masters of Distraction," C 9.

37. Wolf, *Proust and the Squid*, 142–46.

38. Plato, *Phaedrus*, 118.

image. There is more skimming than reading. Moreover, we are highly distracted readers these days. A National Endowment for the Arts Study in 2007 found that almost 60 percent of students in grades seven through twelve read while listening to or watching one or more other forms of media.[39] There is increasing scientific data that such distractions are having a negative impact because an "ecosystem of interruption technologies" scatters our attention.[40]

The result of such interruption technologies is that there is mounting evidence that state of the art educational environments employing technologies of interruption are not producing educational improvements despite enormous investments. In theory these technologies let students proceed at their own pace, teach skills needed in the modern economy, and hold the attention of the students better. The Kyrene Arizona School District agreed and extensively employed new communication technologies. For example, students in an English class produced Facebook pages from the perspective of various characters in Shakespeare and picked songs online from Kanye West to represent the views of a lovelorn Slyvius. What is the result of the new forms of instruction? Since the implementation of the state of the art media technology, the test scores in the Kyrene district have stagnated despite a thirty-three million dollar investment.[41]

The problems of the high technology school are not merely limited to one district. A 2007 Study of the National Endowment for the Arts, *To Read or Not to Read*, concluded that students at all levels are spending less time reading printed materials and their reading comprehension skills are eroding. The reading proficiency rates in adults and younger readers were stagnant or declining at all education levels. And as reading for school or pleasure both decline, not surprisingly writing scores are declining as well because there is a direct correlation between the amount of reading and writing abilities.[42]

So what is happening? Neurological science is revealing the sources of the problem. A study in the journal, *Brain Research*, discovered through PET scans taken of young men playing video games repetitively that there was a sharp decrease in their brain glucose metabolism. This

39. NEA, *To Read or Not to Read*, 8.
40. Doctorow, "Writing in the Age of Distraction."
41. Richtel, "In Classroom of the Future, Stagnant Scores," A 1.
42. NEA, *To Read or Not to Read*, 9–16.

decrease suggested that subjects were using fewer brain circuits and fewer neurons per circuit. Imagine the slowing from tens of thousands of hours of such activity.[43]

There is yet another problem. Research studies demonstrates that our brains are capable of being reconfigured depending on the focus of our mental activities because of the neuroplasticity of our brains.[44] Professor Gary Small at the UCLA Memory and Aging Center did an experiment on older adults where he was able to measure the neurological changes of those who were light users of current informational technologies when they were asked to spend an hour a day on the Internet. The prefrontal cortex of their brains became very active in handling short-term or working memory exercises. These areas actually expanded in size.[45] This is one experiment but imagine the collective impact of billions of hours of web surfing on millions of people.

The frequent switching of texts in these media requires constant decisions as to our next click. We can rapidly move between hypertexts (texts that allows us to move through links to other texts) that rapidly take us to new information. The rapid movements through texts and images interrupt any chance of our reading deeply and preserving the information in our long-term memory. Comparative studies demonstrate that people using traditional linear reading retain more information than those accessing web-based hypertext.[46] The Internet may develop certain visual skills, but there is a loss, in the words of the UCLA Professor of Psychiatry, Patricia Greenfield, of "deep processing: mindful knowledge acquisition, inductive analysis, critical thinking, imagination and reflection."[47]

A fundamental problem resides in the structure of our minds. There is a requirement of sufficiently long and intense mental attentiveness for us to make the proteins in our brain cells that are essential for developing long-term memory. These proteins aid a long-term memory process that sharpens our higher-level cognition in the very process of storing and recalling long-term memory.[48] There is another consequence. A highly

---

43. Haier, et al., "Regional Glucose Metabolic Changes," 134–43.

44. Hotz, "As Brains Change So Can IQ," A 3.

45. Small and Vorgan, *iBrain*, 1, 16, 17.

46. Destefano andLeFevre, "Cognitive Load in Hypertext Reading," 1616–41.

47. Greenfield, "Technology and Informal Education," 69–71.

48. Kandel, *In Search of Memory*, 210.

developed long-term memory capacity is essential for our developing meaning from experiences. Today, our brains are too busy jumping from one image, idea, or bullet-point to the next to engage in these long-term memory and cognitive processes.[49]

If this rewiring were not enough, we learn that our brain chemistry is betraying us. An article in the journal *Nature* reveals that the use of a technology, in this case playing a video game, can have the same effect on the brain as alcohol or narcotics. A PET scan of the brains of video game players revealed an increase in the chemical dopamine in the same area of the brain where such chemicals would be released producing an effect of euphoria as if they were abusing a physical substance.[50]

Not surprisingly given the aforementioned scientific research, reading scores in the Internet age are poor. How can reading *Huckleberry Finn* compete with the euphoria of playing Halo? Six million secondary students are reading below grade level. Only about one-half of graduating high school students is ready for college-level reading. It is not fair to place the entire blame of these reading issues on social media. Still, the amount of simplistic content in and the number of hours diverted to these media cannot help but have a significant impact. The costs from such failures are enormous. The shortage of basic literacy skills costs U. S. businesses and educational institutions $16 billion a year.[51]

The current technologies are also helping to deny many of us essential rest. Students in college generally have a deficit only getting seven hours of sleep compared to the nine and a half hours that they need. One study suggests that students with cell phones lose an additional forty-five minutes of sleep because they do not want to miss out on something. They are often on edge about the next connection and response.[52]

Other social connections are negatively impacted by the current communications revolution. The communication age allows us to be anonymous, selecting the images we wish to view and answering only those e-mails and text messages that we wish to answer. We engage in a

49. Klingberg, *The Overflowing Brain*, 72–75; Crowell, "The Neurobiology of Declarative Memory," 76.

50. Koepp, et al., "Evidence for Striatal Dopamine Release During a Video Game," 266–68.

51. ACT, *Reading Between the Lines, What the ACT Reveals About College Readiness in Reading*. www.act.org/research/policymakers/pdf/reading_report.pdf (2006).

52. Rice, "Bleary Eyed Students Can't Stop Texting Even to Sleep, a Researcher Finds," A 13; Baron, *Always On*.

variety of roles with ever-greater speed and carelessness. The rapid playing of so many roles has aided the loss of intimate relationships A 2006 study appearing in the *American Sociological Review* found that the number of friends or family that the average American discussed important matters with declined from 2.94 friends to 2.08 from 1985 to 2004.[53]

A group especially at risk in this new communications era is teenagers. Information technologies consume a large percentage of teenage life since they provide a technological outlet 24/7 for the teenage urge to ceaselessly dwell on their peer group's plans, feelings, activities, gossip, etc. This focus has for many teenagers restricted or eliminated other relations such as those with parents and older mentors and a range of slower but more reflective activities like reading and the news. In an age of unprecedented access to knowledge, Emory University English professor, Mark Bauerlein, in *The Dumbest Generation* concludes, based on the available social science that today's teenagers are "no more learned or skillful than their predecessors, no more knowledgeable, fluent, up-to date, or inquisitive, except in the materials of youth culture."[54]

This communication environment is not particularly hospitable to ancient truths and religious practices. Indeed, the media offensive washes such positions in a cynical acid and refuses to allow special efficacy to anything except forms that can pierce the relentless background noise with new forms of stimulation. In response to the screen culture, one church in Colorado now has game nights where teenagers relentlessly kill on the computer game, "Halo." The youth pastor justifies such games as the necessary bait to lure teenagers to church where they received Christian messages.[55] Is the thrill of virtual slaughter the bait we want to use? There must be a better way.

The Contemplative Response

We must recognize that the media torrent can reduce human beings to largely autonomous creatures that are self-centered and addicted to the constant massaging of our most superficial sensations and desires. We risk a reduction of our capacities for deep thought and contemplation by constantly viewing the bits and fragments of the screen world. The often

53. McPherson, Smith-Lovin, and Brashears, "Social Isolation in America," 353–75.

54. Bauerlein, *The Dumbest Generation*, 9.

55. Richtel, "Thou Shall Not Kill, Except in a Game at Church," A 1, A 20.

feckless and infantilizing dimensions of the messages in the screen world were revealed to Merton when he passed a television and he observed a "commercial that was on: two little figures were dancing around worshipping a roll of toilet paper, chanting a hymn in its honor . . . We have simply lost the ability to see what is right in front of us: things like this need no comment."[56]

Here the problem is that we use television and other forms of media communications often as forms of diversion or what the seventeenth-century French philosopher, Blaise Pascal, termed divertissements. Merton noted that such diversions seek "to anesthetize the individual as individual, and to plunge him in the warm apathetic stupor of a collectivity."[57]

In Merton's lifetime the falsity of the modern world was already taking many forms. Borrowing the idea of "pseudo event" from the historian Daniel Boorstin, Merton detailed their many forms and decried "the come on's, the releases, the statements, the surmises, the slanders, the quarrels, the insults, and the interminable self advertising of the image makers." This was how we created false masks or "simulacrum" around the real events and truths. We could deliver a variety of myths, distortions, and delusions through these "pseudo events." They nurtured the idols of the modern world where claims of humaneness hid callous, cruel, and cynical objectives.[58]

Merton was also aware that communications media had the capability of locking us into a world of information where we can become very comfortable, perhaps even sedate, in what we view, read, or hear on our screens. In our own age we imagine ourselves as objective and thoughtful citizens of our culture as we only connect with those news programs, radio talk shows, blogs, etc. of the good and decent people who are exactly like us. If facts seem to conflict with these images, Merton warned, "then we feel like we are being tempted by the devil, and we determine that we will be all the more blindly loyal to our images." We are indeed very loyal to the idols of our "slogans and pseudo-events."[59]

If Merton skewered the idols of television, imagine what he would think of the current flood of superficial messages coursing from a host of information technologies. Merton realized in his own day the possibility

56. Merton, Merton, *CT*, 72, "Letter to Czelaw Milosz" (March 28, 1961).
57. Merton, *DQ*, 178.
58. Merton, *FV*, 150–53.
59. Merton, *FV*, 154–55.

of distraction by various forms as advertisers, governments, and other purveyors of slogans that adopted transient and superficial communication forms. These forms of communication hindered our ability to reflect slowly and carefully. We yielded to the demands of the mass society.

> If, when thought is needed, nobody does any thinking, if everyone assumes that someone else is thinking, then it is clear that no one is thinking either for himself or for anybody else. Instead of thought there is a vast, inhuman void, full of words, formulas, slogans, declarations, echoes, ideologies! . . . Nothing can take the place of thoughts. If we do not think, we cannot act freely; we are at the mercy of forces, which we never understand, forces that are arbitrary, destructive, blind, fatal to us and our world.[60]

What was the antidote for Merton? We must oppose communication technologies like television that fostered "a descent to a sub-natural passivity" when the goal should be a "supremely active passivity in understanding and love." Such technologies will not lead to sapiential wisdom or the transcendent. Hence, Merton urged a rejection of the mental numbing by the media because a man must "renounce the passivity of a subject that merely sits and "takes in" what was told him whether in a class or in front of a TV. Part of the cure was "serious and independent reading, and it also means articulate discussion."[61]

An active response must also include substantial civic and spiritual communities where the mental ecology would be more compatible with a contemplative life. We must redevelop our sense of community with neighbors, parishes, civic associations, clubs, and families. Instead of autonomy, solidarity should be our watchword. Merton provided other antidotes to this cultural affliction such as reviving the measured and creative craft traditions like those of the Shakers that will be discussed in chapter 5.[62] Such traditions help to foster a true community.

The most powerful antidote, however, is contemplation. It is in the moments of quiet reflection and prayer that the loud hum of the 24/7 media buzz invading our senses is lowered and the soul can seek comfort, rest, and connection to the divine. Admittedly, the path will not be easy. The call to superficial diversions, so prominent in our world, is

60. Merton, *CGB*, 79.
61. Merton, *WF*, 169, "Letter to Mr. L. Dickson" (September 12, 1965).
62. Flournoy, "Thomas Merton and the Shakers," 7–11.

problematic because they block our connection, in Merton's words, to our "inmost truth—the image of God in [our] own soul."[63]

Merton offered some guidance to mitigate and perhaps elude these contemporary traps. First, we must develop a vital prayer life. Prayer is difficult because we are comfortable with the glitzy, constantly mutating images in our daily media deluge. In contemplative prayer, there is a move away from images and sounds. Instead, we must focus our attention on the mystery that is the "presence of God and . . . His will and His love." We will not be given exact images or sets of images, as that would be a form of idolatry. Indeed, God is "infinitely beyond our comprehension." It is only through a purgation of all objects such as images that we can recognize the divine in reality beyond our nothingness.[64]

In Merton's reflections on contemplation, he emphasized the value of meditative prayer or prayer of the heart. Such prayers were "a way of resting in him whom we have found, who loves, who is near us, who comes to us to draw us to himself." This form of prayer required the finding of a person's deepest center, an awakening in our deepest being to the presence of God. The climate for this type of prayer was one of "awareness and gratitude and a totally obedient love that seeks nothing but to love God." Solitude was critical here so that there was a void that can then be filled by God's presence. We must put aside the "emptiness and futility" of those forms of "distraction and useless communication" which did not contribute to a life of prayer. Hence, we must limit our use of modern communication technologies.[65]

There were still other dimensions of prayer at odds with the frenetic, streaming messages overloading our consciousness. The daily monastic practice of lectio divina involved the four steps of reading, meditation, prayer, and contemplation. The first three steps were sequential and the fourth allows us to rest in God. Merton noted that the goal of these steps was to "call to mind divine truths" while praying in God. Lectio divina drew on the positive dimensions of silence as "the presence of Him who is not heard, so that when all the confused sounds and trivial noises are hushed, then the eloquent voice of reality, of God Himself makes itself heard in peacefulness and in silence." In the silence lectio divina tapped into the wisdom of the "hidden wholeness" and revealed who God was,

---

63. Merton, *DQ*, 183.

64. Merton, *HGL*, 63–64, "Letter to Abdul Aziz" (January 2, 1966).

65. Merton, *Contemplative Prayer*, 32–38; *Praying the Psalms*, 10.

the nature of our relationship to other human beings, and the mystery of salvation.[66]

Through these forms of prayer, we could rewire our brains to accommodate this activity. Because we have become accustomed to slick and entertaining communications, the contemplative prayer life at first may seem boring, empty, and dry. Moreover, Merton recognized that prayer life was not terribly productive in our current sense of the term. Progress in our prayer life was not sequential.

> In technology you have this horizontal progress, where you must start at one point and move to another and then another. But that is not the way to build a life of prayer. In prayer we discover what we already have. You start where you are and you deepen what you already have, and you realize that you are already there. We already have everything, but we don't know it and we don't experience it. Everything has been given to us in Christ. All we need is to experience what we already possess.[67]

Thus, in our prayer life we must be willing to release our false sense of control. In the end, progress in this endeavor was not totally within our command. It came from God's grace, a free gift of the divine. We could prepare for the gift by emptying ourselves and asking for it, but we could not dictate where or when we received grace. So, we may not be thrilled with Merton's suggestion that "progress in prayer comes from the Cross and humiliation and whatever makes us really experience our total poverty and nothingness, and also gets our mind off ourselves."[68] The false self fostered by a sense of autonomy and the endless diversions of our communications culture must be transformed in order to permit our connection to the transcendent.

The modern technological world and its communication forms have lost the best part of life, the access to a more profound vision that encompasses both temporal and spiritual realities. As part of this vision, our contemplative connection with the divine is a very special gift. This divine gift is not a matter of our intellectual or physical labors; it is not the product of a special technique. This is a form of awareness of how God operated or to use a word favored by Saint Thomas Aquinas, "played" throughout the world, a world of divine festivity. If we are open to this

---

66. Merton, *Monastic Observances*, 155; Merton, "Lectio Divina," 5–10.

67. Steindl-Rast, "Man or Prayer," 80.

68. Merton, *HGL*, 376, "Letter to Etta Gullick" (April 6, 1966).

reality, Merton revealed that we could occupy "a space of freedom, of true learning, of attunement to the world-as-a-whole."[69]

Living With a Dull Roar

While Merton's approach and insights may be correct, our age presents a variety of challenges for the digital self. How can we live thoughtfully in a culture of distraction? There is little time for sustained reflection on anything. Our culture has us thinking in fragments as we watch streams of constantly mutating images. The resulting confusion in our mental operations does not allow us to effectively parse complex issues or to experience deep spiritual truths.

How do we contemplate in such a world? As Merton well knew, we must provide prophetic resistance and we must seek allies. The prophetic resistance must take on a missionary task, especially to a generation of millennials who have not experienced the world before the screen age. Their world has always had personal computers, cell phones, and the Internet. In the words of a young Franciscan theologian, Daniel Horan, OFM, they are "digital natives" who suffer from emotional instability, a lack of interpretive control, a loss of embodiment, and are driven by the needs of instant gratification. They also have a crisis of identity about their vocation or higher calling.[70]

The good news about the millennials is that the search for a spiritual self is alive; surveys indicate millennials want a spiritual life and authenticity. To this end Merton offers antidotes to the false self that is too often nurtured in the digital world. For Merton, the false self or exterior self can create any number of false images of our selves. Horan notes, however, that we have resources in the contemplative tradition to renew our encounter with reality, with God. For example, the excessive speed and immediacy of the screen age needs to be countered by the space and time needed to be with God. Horan concludes that "millennials in their search for the true self would be well served to recall the words of Francis of Assisi, someone Thomas Merton always revered and held as an example

69. Merton, Review of *In Tune with the World*, 108–9.

70. Horan, OFM, "Striving Towards Authenticity," 80–89. I was aided here by listening to a lecture by Father Horan, "Digital Natives and the Digital Self" at a conference at Bellarmine University sponsored by the Thomas Merton Center, titled, "Contemplation in a Technological Era: Merton's Insight for the Twenty-First Century."

of sanctity, who wrote to his brothers, 'What a person is before God, that he is and no more.'"[71]

The prophetic role is not just for theologians and spiritual writers. Merton also believed there were secular writers and intellectuals that he termed vitalists who sensed the elements of falsity and inhumanity in technology. Don DeLillo in his novel, *White Noise*, whose characters suffer from being in the midst of two much noise, too much distraction, too much sensation of the modern technological world that is subject to a "dull and unlocatable roar." DeLillo was writing in 1985, before the onslaught of many of our 24/7 devices and capabilities had invaded our world. What DeLillo described as a "dull and unlocatable roar" is now a category five hurricane of noise. But the problem is not just external; it is internal. We are part of the problem. We are in the grip of a strange compulsion to relentlessly communicate. One of Merton's observations was on point here: "How tragic it is that they who have nothing to express are continually expressing themselves, like nervous gunners, firing burst after burst of ammunition into the dark where there is no enemy . . . They chatter themselves to death, fearing life as if it were death."[72]

There will also be some allies in strange places, among the enclaves of high technology. In his own day, Merton connected with Leo Szilard, one of the makers of the atomic bomb. In our day, consider Sherry Turkle, who is a professor at MIT and director of the MIT Initiative on Technology and Self. Professor Turkle has tracked the impact of communication technologies since the 1980s as a trained clinical psychologist. In her book, *Alone Together*, she notes how these technologies have evolved from simple isolated units to being complex and interconnected. In this evolutionary process, we have evolved as well to be able to shape online identities. Our self has become less integrated and more protean. There have been other losses. We objectify other people; we are less intimately connected. Turkle cites as an example the online program Chatroulette that allows the user to be randomly connected to others around the world. People generally hit next after a few seconds. People are "objectified and quickly discarded." Such technological screening of human connections allows us to avoid intimacy and its discontents.[73]

---

71. Ibid., 89.

72. Merton, *No Man Is an Island*, 162.

73. Turkle, *Alone Together*, xiv.

For Turkle, there are other losses in a digital world. We not only lose intimacy, but also authenticity. We no longer have to deal with messy emotional embodied realities that directly confront us. We are drawn to the "comfort of connections without the demands of intimacy." And yet we are not happy in this universe. We are disoriented, anxious, and paradoxically alone amidst all the connection. She also concludes in words that Merton would have understood and approved, "if we are always on we may deny ourselves the rewards of solitude."[74]

Once we realize the problem and that our potential resources including secular allies, we can embark on a life that is in some senses a counter-cultural protest. We can refuse to become aimless chips floating on the sea of a collective society and its slogans and images. Merton reminded us that we were called to such a prophetic task if we were to follow our destiny as children of God and creators of truth, beauty, and meaning.

In this quest, the answer was not necessarily to completely abandon the information age. Merton came to realize that technology was inevitable in some form and could often be desirable as long as we remember that, "Technology can elevate and improve man's life only [if] it remains subservient to his real interests; that it respects his true being; that it remembers that the origin and goal of all being is in God."[75]

We can pursue a lifestyle consistent with this understanding if we slow our pace when and where we can, join embodied communities, and accept the value and efficacy of a deep prayer life. We could make different choices; we could cut back on the 200 billion hours a year that we as a nation spend watching television and use part of this "cognitive surplus" for deep reading.[76] For example, Merton observed that "there is nothing to prevent a layman from taking just one Psalm a day, for instance in his night prayers, and reciting it thoughtfully, pausing to meditate on the lines which have the deepest meaning for him."[77]

We must be creative in restoring a sense of spiritual vitality as walls of sound and data, the thick white noise of our media world, encircle us. These walls are ones that Merton would recognize, for he too lived in an age of falsity and "special searching and questioning." Such an age

74. Turkle, *Alone Together*, 3.
75. Merton, *CGB*, 230.
76. Shirky, *Cognitive Surplus*, 27.
77. Merton, *Praying the Psalms*, 14.

needed meditation and prayer, because only prayers of "humble supplication" could turn our despair into a "perfect hope."[78] With meditation and prayer, we can traverse the media walls. This action is not a physical action, but is an inner spiritual journey. This is one of the unique callings of our age. In the end, as Saint Augustine observed, we can feel the transcendent pull and respond in prayer because our hearts are restless until they rest in God.

And what advice might we give to Mr. Campbell, our media addicted friend mentioned at the beginning of the chapter? Merton might warn him using the words of the Taoist philosopher, Chuang Tzu, that, "He who is controlled by objects, loses possession of his inner self." Mr. Campbell might want to recognize the damage to his life from his addiction to information technologies. He needs to balance his use of technology and employ self-management techniques that allow for regular meals, exercise, and times for relaxation.[79] He should have technology-free days every Saturday and Sunday and measure his time spent on real reflection or in spontaneous play with others versus the hours spent on information technologies. Some experts on communication technologies offer additional tips. Mr. Campbell should check e-mail messages once an hour at most and focus on only one task at a time, perhaps while listening to soothing background music to improve concentration. He should not drive and talk while on a cell phone or while texting.[80] Also, don't forget your family. No success at work is worth failure at home. Put down your computer and play with your children. These are just a few small steps towards balancing a life between the demands of modern communication technologies and what we require to be fully human.

78. Merton, *Contemplative Prayer*, 25–28.

79. Zimmerman, "Distracted," B 8.

80. Lohr, "Slow Down Brave Multitasker, and Don't Read This in Traffic."

CHAPTER 4

Choosing to be Human or Transhuman

I and many other scientists now believe that in around 20 years we will have the means to reprogram our bodies' stone-age software so we can halt, then reverse, aging. Then nanotechnology will let us live forever.

Ray Kurzweil, author, inventor, and futurist
in *Nanotechnology Law Report* (2009)

I praise you because I am wonderfully made; wonderful are your works!

Psalm 139:14.

On the Eve of a Revolution

WE ARE BEGINNING A biotechnological revolution. Consider these headlines from major new sources in the United States over the last five years.

- "Is the Key to Creativity in Your Pillbox or in Your PC?"

- "'Wombs for Rent': the Latest Job Outsourcing to India"

- "Assembling the Global Baby"

- "How a Drug Can Target Your Worst Memories and Erase Them Forever"

- "Mice Are Created from Two Males"

- "Merging Man and Machine: The Bionic Age"
- "Scientists Build a Rat Lung in a Laboratory"
- "Cell Study Finds Way to Slow the Ravages of Age"
- "Closing in on the Formula for Artificial Skin"[1]

These headlines suggest that we are on the verge of making unprecedented changes in human biology because of an array of new technologies. These technologies suggest we are on the verge of a startling possibility, the creation of a new human form—the transhuman.

Should there be any limits to our advances? We are making rules for unprecedented capabilities as we go along. For example, on the issue of part human and part animal chimeras, a few years ago the *Washington Post* reported that Dr. Stuart Weisman at the Stanford Institute of Regenerative Medicine injected brain cells from aborted fetuses into the brains of fetal mice, so that the mouse's brain would be mostly human. The goal was to allow testing on the brain cells that could not be done in humans. The head of the Stanford ethics committee stated that the experiments would stop if the mice show human behaviors like "improved memory or problem solving."[2]

We are also on the verge of transforming our mental reality in a fundamental way. There are experiments under way suggesting that we will soon be able to radically alter our memories, deleting unwanted memories. The basic premise in these experiments is that we use proteins to build memories. When we recall a specific memory we use proteins to recall the memory. By blocking the protein with a chemical inhibitor, we break the circuit for recalling that memory. It is gone. Of course, this blocking can be used for any memory. Proponents argue that this technique is like using pain medication to eliminate physical suffering.[3] Is this really the same? What is lost through this technique?

The mouse/human brain and the memory pill suggest that for the first time in our history we may soon be able to radically transform and

1. Zachary, "Is the Key to Creativity in Your Pillbox or in Your PC," B3; Audi and Chang, "Assembling the Global Baby," C1; Lehrer, "The Forgetting Pill," 84–93, 120; Naik, "Mice Are Created From Two Males," A8; National Geographic Society, "Merging Man and Machine"; Naik, "Scientists Build a Rat Lung in a Lab," A3; Wang, "Cell Study Finds a Way to Slow the Ravages of Age," A2; Wang, "Closing in on the Formula for Artificial Skin," D3.

2. Weiss, "Human Brain Cells Grow in Mice."

3. Lehrer, "The Forgetting Pill," 84–93, 120.

perhaps even transcend the very nature of our species. This astonishing prospect of human transformation has been termed transhumanism. When I use this term, I am referring to a wide range of biotechnologies that will enable a radical evolution of human biology beyond its current capacities and limitations. At some point, we may no longer be human in the current sense; we will have transformed ourselves into a new entity—the transhuman.[4] There are two aspects to my assessment of transhumanism. First, I will outline the potentially dangerous trajectory for biotechnology on the issues of reproductive manipulation and the extension of human life in the coming years. Then, I want to consider how we might evaluate such possibilities through a contemplative critique based on Thomas Merton's work.

So let me begin with the current trajectory of biotechnology. Gregory Stock, director of the Program on Medicine, Technology, and Society at UCLA Medical School, has declared that the developing capacities of genetic modification signals "the beginning of human self design."[5] Going a step further, Dr. Steven Potter, Professor in the Department of Developmental Biology at Children's Hospital Medical Center in Cincinnati, recognizes that we will soon "have complete control of our genetic destiny that could well mean the end of the human species as we know it."[6]

These comments reveal that what was just a few decades ago fantastic and unthinkable are in some instances becoming live possibilities. Still, we must be careful not to be drawn excessively to the grotesque, the dramatic, and the idiosyncratic in our analysis. Tales of a future with headless clones harvested for their organs, militaristic robotic legions or android courtesans may increase the readership of magazines or books, but we will probably avoid such obvious dangers as we regulate our technologies in our own self-interest.[7]

4. The term transhumanism is used in many ways. I am focusing on its eugenic character that seeks the radical transformation and perfection of the human person. When I Googled transhumanism, there were 261,000 hits demonstrating its impact and scope. There are numerous transhumanism societies, books, articles, and manifestoes.

5. Stock, *Redesigning Humans*, 3.

6. Potter, *Designer Genes*, 175.

7. The headless clone concerns began with experiments creating headless clones of frogs. Associated Press, "Scientist Creates Headless Frog Embryos in Laboratory," 26A; There were even learned academic discussions of this phenomena. Mosteller, "Aristotle and Headless Clones," 339–350; On fears of a robot revolution overtaking humanity, see Joy, "Why the Future Doesn't Need Us"; Levy, *Love and Sex With Robots*.

Legislative bodies and regulatory agencies should also be prudent in not sponsoring premature legislation. I am thinking here, for example, of a proposed Georgia statute to forbid the implantation of a chip in the human brain without consent. California, North Dakota, and Wisconsin have passed similar bills.[8] Such premature regulation can undermine the credibility of the very institutions that will at the right moment need to prohibit or regulate such technologies. This precipitous legislation may violate the balance between Rickover's rules, cited by Merton, that:

1) A technology must be assessed in advance as to its potential for harm. The technology should not be applied until it can be rendered harmless;

2) Authorities should consult and listen carefully to the advice of their experts.

It is not premature, however, for the Georgia legislature or relevant state agencies to study this issue. More than a dozen laboratories in the United States are working on brain/computer interfaces. A brain chip has been used to allow a man with a spinal injury to feed his brain signals into a computer that deciphers his thoughts and works with software that allows him to control devices in his house. The device, called BrainGate, allows him to turn his television on and off and change channels merely by his thoughts working through this system.[9] This line of research offers wonderful possibilities for the estimated 500 million people in the world who suffer from physical, sensory, and mental impairments.

The danger? A mind-reading brain chip may one day hold out the possibility of ethical violations. What if we could reverse the flow and feed information into the brain? But this possibility is not on the immediate horizon; there is no evidence of any plan for nonconsensual brain chip implantation. When and if there is such a possibility then the regulation of such devices will be necessary. Currently, the Rickover requirements are not met by the Georgia statute because the dangerous technology does not yet exist, much less is it being implanted without consent. At this point, the legislation still seems more than a little fanciful. One legislator in Georgia labeled the proposed bill, "a solution looking for a problem."[10]

8. Georgia Senate Bill 230, "The Microchip Consent Act of 2010"; Greenblat, "Lawmakers Are Working on Anti-Brain-Chip Bill."

9. Martin, "Mind Control"; Gnanayutham, et al., "Discrete Acceleration and Personalized Tiling," 261–70.

10. Greenblat, "Lawmakers Are Working on Anti-Brain-Chip Bill." One witness

Having proposed some important caveats, let us evaluate a couple of biotechnologies that have the potential to radically alter human life. One avenue for this kind of progress is through the genetic engineering of children. We can already select for gender and other traits through genetic testing and the elimination of "defective" embryos from in vitro fertilization. How far do we want to pursue genetic modifications? Modifications that eliminate cancer and other diseases are highly desirable. Such procedures will help to maintain our natural state of health. The perfecting of human beings, also known as eugenics, however, aims not at avoiding disease but desires to perfect our biological and psychic natures. We can already avoid having disabled children through genetic testing of the embryo followed by abortion, but even many reproductive rights advocates are uneasy with the use of abortion for eugenic purposes.[11] There are troubling questions. How far do we go with our search for perfection? Do we want to just work on physical features or do we also include intelligence and personality traits?

Finally, we may be able to remove one of the great limitations of our biology, our mortality. As we perfect our physical and mental features and life experiences, many transhumanists desire to conquer death as well. Our life spans are at least partly the result of the fact that most cells have a limited ability to continuously divide and create new cells. There is a race among biotechnology companies to overcome this limitation. At a minimum, this research may extend our life spans by several decades over the next century and some, like the futurist Ray Kurzweil, predict no limits on human life expectancy in the near future. Kurzweil has the ear of many in Silicon Valley. On the back cover of his book, *The Singularity is Near*, Bill Gates gushes, "Ray Kurzweil is the best person I know at predicting the future of artificial intelligence. His intriguing new book envisions a future in which information technologies have advanced so far and fast that they enable humanity to transcend its biological limitations—transforming our lives in ways which we can't yet imagine."[12] Indeed.

---

on a hearing on the Georgia bill claimed she had a device implanted in her vaginal-rectum area by the Department of Defense. Galloway, "Delusions, The Legislature and an Implanted Microchip."

11. Harmon, "Genetic Testing +Abortion=???" *New York Times*, sec. 4, 1, 4.

12. Kurzweil, *The Singularity Is Near*, 210–215.

The Power of the Bioindustrial Complex

Is there anything problematic about our transhumanist future? After all, transhumanism affirms some of our deep-seated cultural assumptions. It will expand the range of our individual choices and add to the utility of our lives. It may deliver higher IQs, longer lives, and less crime.

The ethical guardians, the bioethicists, will generally desire to regulate this process, but will provide no fundamental opposition to these developments. The theoretical framework of most bioethicists will insure such a stance. Most of these ethicists have adopted some mid-level form of ethical principles that operates between case studies and foundational ethical or religious belief systems. The mid-level's most famous proponents are Tom Beauchamp and James Childress, whose book, *Principles of Biomedical Ethics*, has enormously influenced the discipline of applied ethics. They apply four key ethical criteria—justice, nonmaleficence, beneficence, and autonomy to their case studies.[13] These principles are quite useful in assessing, for example, a new medical therapy. They insure that any technology or procedure must consider the importance of patients having full knowledge of procedures and access to comparable resources regardless of wealth. Their terminology of ethical values allows those operating from different religious, cultural, and political backgrounds to find some common ground for resolving standard medical or bioethical issues.

The coming waves of biotechnologies will be able to alter human life in heretofore unimaginable ways and ethicists may need to do more than offer a regulatory regime. Lori Andrews, the director of the Institute for Science, Law, and Technology at Chicago-Kent College of Law and a longtime advocate of reproductive rights, raises a troubling question for them: "Should anything be allowable so long as a lawyer can come up with a scheme to deal with it? Or are there some scientific 'advances' that would so change the nature of our society (or so waste money or damage the participants) that they should be prohibited?"[14] In regard to genetic engineering, most bioethicists like Arthur Caplan will conclude that "in so far as coercion and force are absent and individual choice is allowed to hold sway, then presuming fairness in the access to the means of enhancing our offspring, it is hard to see what is wrong with trying to create more perfect babies or more perfect adults."[15]

13. Beauchamp and Childress, *Principles of Biomedical Ethics*, 12–23.
14. Andrews, *The Clone Age*, 5.
15. Caplan, "What's Morally Wrong with Eugenics?" 222.

Indeed, what could be more American than improving ourselves or our children? We are a nation that loves progress, improvement, and innovation. Plastic surgeries, self-help books, steroids, accent reduction clinics, and many other procedures and services reveal our insatiable appetite for self-improvement.[16] There is already survey data that confirms that a growing percentage of Americans are very comfortable with genetic modifications. Entrepreneurs are prepared to meet their needs. A Los Angeles clinic, Fertility Institutes, has refined pre-implantation genetic diagnosis to the point that it could select for a variety of traits like gender and eye color. In response to some criticism, the director, Jeff Steinberg, counters that, "This is cosmetic medicine."[17] Moreover, there could be enormous economic benefits for transhumanism as part of an expanding biotechnology industry. According to industry analysts Ernst and Young, biotechnology companies in the developed world had profits of $3.7 billion dollars in 2009.[18]

Given what I have described, those who wish to seriously question the ends of transhumanism will be opposed by an organized bioindustrial complex of corporations, academic researchers, and bioethicists who will spend enormous time and money appealing to individual choice, economic prosperity, and a mild regulatory regime to foster popular support for their vision. The bioindustrial complex will make opposing a biotechnology-based eugenics a very difficult proposition.

The path to this future will in all likelihood be much different than the eugenics of the early twentieth century that employed involuntary sterilization. In the future, eugenics will probably be voluntary and not state-imposed. It might well come in a form like that in the movie, *Gattaca* (1997). In the future world depicted by this film, the genetic modification of embryos is voluntary, but to forgo genetic modifications is to doom one's child to manual labor. The protagonist, Vincent, is a "natural," born without genetic modification who is employed cleaning buildings but dreams of being an astronaut. Vincent assumes the identity of Jerome Morrow, a genetically engineered perfect human who is a paraplegic as a result of a car accident. Vincent learns how to use Jerome's blood and urine to deceive the testing at the space agency and begins his training as an astronaut. In the end, Vincent realizes his dream.

16. An excellent book on our national obsession for perfecting ourselves is Elliot, *Better Than Well.*

17. Naik, "A Baby, Please," A10.

18. Ernst and Young, "Biotech industry showing resilience."

In *Gattaca*, genetic determinism scars the main characters in the movie who suffer from their sense of being determined by their genetic heritage. It ruins family and other personal relationships. It creates impenetrable class divisions. We are also reminded through the heroic success of the genetically deficient protagonist that our genetic content, although important, is not destiny. Are we headed for a world like Gattaca? Time will tell, but there are strong economic and cultural forces favoring such an outcome.

A Contemplative Critique

Having outlined some serious problems with the development and use of an array of emerging biotechnologies, let us bring Merton's contemplative principles into the discussion. On the issue of perfecting ourselves through genetics, Merton recognized that there were serious implications for humanity in the emerging field of genetics still in its infancy at his death. He confided in 1967 that genetic mutations from x-rays might be a harbinger of a "drastic genetic change in the near future." He proposed that leadership be exerted to control this new technical capacity so it would not be employed "haphazardly." He declared that "once again it becomes imperative that there be some concerted action by the best minds everywhere to control this power in view of the interests of man."[19] Human reflection, at its most profound depths, must frame the discussion about genetics.

Instead, we too often approach medical issues with a detached objectivity. Merton encountered this mentality in his hospital visits. He was thankful for medical care, but the hospitals were institutions of a "totally alien country" where long bouts of passivity were broken by unannounced medical interventions. Teams of medical providers arranged "ingenious and complicated happenings."[20] He was prodded, poked, and probed in a "medieval frenzy." Doctors had a "remarkable flair for improvisation on people's backs, elbows, guts, etc." Only the human contact of nurses and friends helped to mitigate the worst aspects of these invasions.[21]

19. Merton, *LL*, 244.
20. Merton, *DWL*, 102, entry of May 8, 1964.
21. Merton, *The School of Charity*, 332, "Letter to Father John Eudes Bamberger" (May 4, 1967); Merton, *RJ*, 153–54, "Letter to Robert Lax" (March, 1940); Hartford, *Merton and Friends*, 86.

This detached and objective approach is also evident in our development of new biotechnologies. Let us examine one form of genetic manipulation and self-design that is close to being realized in our own age, which is the possibility of cloning another human being. I am not referring to therapeutic cloning for stem cells here, but the cloning of another full human being that is a genetic replica of the donor. The act of cloning poses deep anthropological questions. For example, what does it mean to be a fully human person? Many who defend cloning invoke its potential utility to a parent who cannot conceive or a grieving parent who can recreate a lost child. The zoologist and expert on evolution, Richard Dawkins, has wondered if cloning would allow a form of self-perfection and observes, "I find it a personally riveting thought that I could watch a small copy of myself, fifty years younger and wearing a baseball hat instead of a British Empire pith helmet, nurtured through the early decades of the twenty first century. Mightn't it feel almost like turning back your personal clock fifty years? And mightn't it be wonderful to advise your junior copy on where you went wrong, and how to do it better?"[22]

Dawkins' comments are indicative of how the drive for human perfection and control of our biological destiny nurtures problematic desires and outcomes. Instead of relating to others, especially his child as a special gift of creation, Merton, I believe, would hold that Dawkins is intent on cloning a copy to affirm himself and his "own limited needs and desires." Other people are "real only insofar as they can be related to these selfish desires."[23]

For Merton, this narcissism partakes of the problem of agreeing to an abstract concept of the human as an object for manipulation. The needs of human technological progress present one form of this tendency to abstraction that ignores the individual person as a free and concrete human being that we relate to with compassion, love, and mercy. This explains why "modern secular humanisms are so fair and optimistic in theory and so utterly merciless and inhuman in practice."[24]

Let me present a cautionary historical example of this paradox that should be a warning against naively adopting all of the "gifts" offered by the bioindustrial complex. There was a movement among many progressive voices, including Woodrow Wilson and Theodore Roosevelt, to

22. Dawkins, "What's Wrong with Cloning?" 54–66.
23. Merton, *LL*, 146.
24. Ibid., 148–49.

improve the "stock" of the United States in the early twentieth century. There were too many unfit mothers and children; the good of the nation was at risk from immigrants, hillbillies, blacks, loose women, and others deemed unfit. Armed with a theory of eugenics based on a simplistic genetic model and the assumptions of social utility and Social Darwinism, an involuntary sterilization campaign against the unfit had the support of all the major political parties, classes, sections of the country, and professions. The Supreme Court in *Buck v. Bell* (1927) in an 8–1 decision upheld an involuntary sterilization law, on the basis of very slight evidence, declaring, "three generations of imbeciles is enough." Thirty-seven states then adopted involuntary sterilization laws. Sterilizations were performed recklessly based on little or no evidence. At first, the only consistent opponents to such laws were Catholics and some fundamentalists. The Nazis' blatant copying of such sterilization laws, the advance of genetic science that contradicted the claims of the eugenicists, and a growing sense of sexual privacy combined to cause the abandonment of sterilization laws by the late 1960s.[25] Why was this terrible invasion of reproductive rights allowed? As Merton would have recognized, an abstract ideal of progress embraced by the learned and the caring was inhumane in practice.

In order to be human, Merton believed a person must not construct a false self or pursue unjust laws justified by their utility or the goal of perfecting humanity. Cloning could allow human beings to be constantly refined like cattle to preserve certain traits for particular tasks. In our technological hubris, we are "imperiled by man's pride and deranged self-love." This is the "strong temptation" of secular progress. Merton's concern was not with technological creativity per se but its tendency to serve an idol of power instead of divine love. Society should affirm the inherent dignity of each human being and their ineffable reality in a "total vocation." This "total vocation" must seek the purposes of God and "the genuine good of the human race"; we must give ourselves to our brothers and sisters in a service of love in which "God will manifest his creative power through men on earth."[26]

Despite these arguments, the proponents of cloning may counter with the difficult case. What about the benefits to the childless couple from cloning? In many cases, current technologies can resolve infertility.

---

25. Thompson, "Silent Protest: A Catholic Justice Dissents in *Buck v. Bell*," 125–48.

26. Merton, "Technology," 57–58; Merton, *LL*, 149–50.

But in the unresolved situations, hard cases should not make a bad law; hard cases should not override ethical concerns. Employing Rickover's rules, the case of a cloning of a childless parent is a violation of weighing the long range common good of a society against the short-term advantage to the parents. Moreover, if such a couple was granted its wish, cloning could endanger the psychic health of the cloned person by violating their sense of individuality and uniqueness. What is the psychic impact of being haunted by the memory or physical presence of a person who is you but is older? If the donor had an onset of an inherited disease, what would be the psychic impact on the clone?

These questions are reminders that those who make the decision for cloning cannot consult in advance the person most affected, the clone. Applying Rickover's third principle, the liberty of the scientists and the "parent" end when their choices harm the freedom of the clone. There is the liberty interest of the cloned person in being free of the potentially crushing psychological burden of being cloned instead of the genetic offspring of two parents. Another problem is an obvious disparity between the parents and the offspring. Will there be an equal connection to both parents? Moreover, how would it feel to be the product of vanity, not love, in many cases? The potential psychological damage resulting from this process is considerable.

Turning from the beginning to the end of human life, what about the prospect of a radical extension of human life? There has already been considerable progress in extending the human life span. A baby born in the United States in 1900 could expect to live forty-seven years and one born in 2010 can expect to live eighty years. A number of futurists claim that we may be on the verge of even more radical breakthroughs in the near term to extend human life. They contend that our biological deterioration is not fixed by our genetics; there is no firm limit to our life span built into the human genome. Aging is a process of cellular destruction that can be minimized today and may one day be eliminated. At this point, the causes of cellular aging are not fully understood, but one key component is the releasing of oxygen or radicals from cellular processes, like sparks from cellular engines, that damages key cell functions and these damaged aspects of cells accumulate over time, causing an increasing decline of the cells' full functioning. This is aging.[27]

27. Weiner, *Long for this World*, 71–81.

Scientists are advancing on many fronts to delay or eliminate the aging process. In this quest, they can access formidable economic resources. With many of the baby boomers looking for a fountain of youth, some questionable products like Botox are producing enormous profits. Billions of dollars are available to be invested in biotechnology research. Many leading gerontologists and cardiologists, according to a RAND Corporation study, are predicting a life-extending compound in the next ten years. The pharmaceutical company Glaxo has already paid $750 million for the rights to resveratol, a compound that slows aging in lab animals. There is obviously a pent-up demand for life preserving technology. Even cryogenics, the highly suspect freezing of bodies for later resuscitation, has spawned a half dozen frozen resting places for those awaiting defrosting and resurrection.[28]

Accessing enormous financial resources, the eternal life agenda might be unveiled in stages. The futurists Ray Kurzweil and Terry Grossman propose a program of extending life starting with our current capabilities to slow aging. Based on his research with Grossman, Kurzweil confesses that he has reprogrammed his biochemistry by taking 250 pill supplements a day. He fine-tunes his intakes based on the measurements of dozens of nutrient levels. The result is that he claims that his fifty-six year old body has a biological age of forty.[29]

Another key proponent of life extension using current technology is the gerontologist, Aubrey de Grey. His basic approach is practical immortality or what he terms, "negligible senescence." For de Grey, the body is like a car and we merely have to keep it in good operating order through maintenance and cleaning and replacement when necessary. Employing these measures, we can last a very long time, perhaps forever. To this end, de Grey calls for funding a war on aging so that we can live in a "new summer of vigor and health, the dark specter of the age plague driven away by the sunshine of perpetual youth."[30]

Advances in current research seem to support the life extending visions of Kurzweil and de Grey. Partially disabling a single gene in tiny worms has doubled their lives. Researchers at the Mayo Clinic have successfully used a drug to target and kill senescent or aging cells in mice. These senescent cells produce harmful toxins that cause medical

28. Weintraub, *Selling the Fountain of Youth*, 213–14; Miller, "Robert Ettinger," A8.

29. Kurzweil and Grossman, *Transcend*, 313–36.

30. de Grey, *Ending Aging*, 101–273, 339.

problems like inflammation and diabetes. The drug, by killing these dangerous cells, essentially freezes aspects of the aging process.[31]

After slowing aging, the next step will be to take advantage of the next wave of biotechnologies, such as genetic therapies, new cancer and heart medicines, and cell replacements. In the more distant future, nanotechnologies will allow us to alter human physiology at the molecular level. With this capacity, we will be able to reverse aging and sever the linkage of calendar time and biological health. Artificial intelligence and robotics are the final step and will allow us to upload our minds into virtually indestructible forms.[32]

Although he was prescient in many ways, Merton could not have comprehended an eternal biological life. Death was, to borrow a phrase from the theologian David Tracy, a limits question. Merton declared that, "There still remain limits where we face the void from which no mechanical rescue is possible. And these limits will never be abolished."[33] Although he may be proven wrong about the limits of our mortality, Merton still offers wisdom on the meaning of death. While death was understandably difficult, it was a point of spiritual challenge, not a technical limit where we defeated the demands of our current biology. Death was the final stage of the challenge of life, which was how to live together in community while also living alone in solitude. In his solitude, the life's work of the contemplative was "to work his way through the darkness of his own mystery until he discovers that his mystery and the mystery of God merge into one reality, which is the only reality." Paradoxically, we faced this prospect alone but in the supportive presence and company of others who can ponder the beauty of life and the mystery of death. In summation, Merton concluded that the dying Christian is "one with the Church, but he also suffered the agony of Christ's death in Gethsemani."[34]

This wrestling of the solitary to engage his or her mystery and the mystery of God in death is very different than the idea of a technological victory in a war on death, where in the words of Kurzweil death was always a "calamity." Merton criticized those for whom "death is the enemy who seems to confront them at every moment in the deep darkness and silence of their own being. So they keep shouting at death.

31. Baker, et al., "Clearance of p16ink4a_positive senescent cells"; Arrison, "Living to 100 and Beyond," C1, C2; Arrison, *100 Plus.*

32. Kurzweil, *The Singularity is Near*, 205–54.

33. Merton, "The Angel and the Machine," 6.

34. Merton, *DQ*, 180–81.

They confound their lives with noise. They stun their own ears with meaningless words, never discovering that their hearts are rooted in a silence that is not death but life."[35]

For Merton death was a companion, a reminder of the barrier between the human and the divine.[36] It was not the end of human reality; it was in fact a point of departure to an ultimate communion with the divine that was the goal of the contemplative. So he could tell a sister that she was right to grieve over the loss of a fellow nun but it was even more correct to celebrate the "joy" that the departed was now experiencing.[37] Merton thus balanced a realization of the psychology of loss with the ultimate claims of the faith. In another letter he could both commiserate with and console a friend who lost a loved one, "It is natural for you to feel terribly lonely and upset. Death is a terrible thing, . . . But when you come face to face with it, there is nothing you can do or say. It is final. That is why you feel so lost about it. But yet, our faith tells us, it is not final in God's eyes. For man, it is the end. For man in Christ it is just the beginning."[38]

As Merton indicated, there was a great hope that transcended the passing of a person's mortal existence. To cling to the notion of an eternal temporal life was a claim of the autonomous modern man. It is the same problem in a new form that he had denounced in "Atlas and the Fat Man." It was part of a domination mentality that had destroyed and poisoned the environment. Kurzweil and de Grey employed this mentality of control on behalf of an idolization of the human experience. And while our health and our lives are important, they should not be valued as an end in themselves, an idol.

Kurzweil and de Grey also present a flawed anthropology. For them, the highest end of the human person is our ability to transform ourselves even into a new entity. There is a fundamental pathology in their wishing to perfect themselves and conquer death. For Merton, the root of this pathology was a "metaphysical solitude" that provoked a terror that we had no meaning or reality. So in our weakness within the walls of our fear we sought to snatch some love, knowledge, or power from one another. Or we rebel. This was the Promethean error.

---

35. Merton, *No Man is an Island*, 262.

36. Kurzweil, *The Singularity Is Near*, 210.

37. Merton, *WF*, 188, "Letter to Sister Anita" (January 1, 1962).

38. Ibid., 251, "Letter to William Robert Miller" (April 10, 1965).

We defied our plight and in our despair we attempted to transcend our reality through our own efforts. Enter Kurzweil and de Grey, who seek to perfect humanity through life extension.

Our ability to technologically control our environment leads these two to the illusion that they can control everything. They are subject to the common illusion that we are "rich enough, powerful enough, and clever enough to cheat death."[39] For Merton the paradox is that "the only way we become perfect is by leaving ourselves, and, in a sense, forgetting our own perfection, to follow Christ."[40] Our main task is not refashioning our bodies but to "live in full and vital awareness of this ground of my being and the world's being."[41] In death we are returning to the source of our being and our deepest love. Merton concluded that, "Death is the point at which life can obtain its pure fulfillment" and it "brings life to its goal. But the goal is not death; it is life."[42] In the final analysis, if we fight death day and night, we are not living a fully human life. Why? Instead of succumbing to this illusion, we can proceed in dignity and with less anxiety by adopting the freedom to accept and face death as a natural part of the human experience and our ultimate destiny.

Seeking Allies, Making Careful Judgments

About a decade ago, I was at a Texas Senate hearing on the issue of stem cell research. A panel of four or five "experts" representing universities, economists, biotechnology companies, research laboratories, and bio-ethics centers presented reams of glossy documents and well-articulated reasons for promoting embryonic stem cell research as the key to future medical breakthroughs. The panel suggested that to reject such research was to consign millions to the horrors of a score of diseases and medical conditions. It also would relegate the state of Texas to being an economic backwater. The well-funded and sophisticated campaign of the bioindustrial complex that I witnessed that day appears to be wrong at this point. Embryonic stem cell research has produced relatively few clinical applications compared to adult stem cell research. Moreover, there is increasing evidence that stem cells can be produced from a variety of

39. Merton, "The Contemplative Life in the Modern World," 224.

40. Merton, *The New Man*, 23–34.

41. Merton, *CGB*, 320.

42. Merton, *LL*, 105.

techniques without destroying embryos. For example, research at Children's Hospital in Boston suggests that skin cells can be turned into stem cells and then these stem cells can be turned into a variety of cells.[43]

The Texas example reveals both the kind of groups and the forms of argument that will be involved in the transhumanism debates. It also demonstrates that the path to transhumanism is once again not inevitable as their legislative proposals were defeated. But, we must prepare the groundwork for a thoughtful opposition. In this opposition, as Merton noted, we must seek allies among "vitalists" who detect the flaws of transhumansim. For example, Kazuo Ishiguro's novel *Never Let Me Go* presents a coming of age story at an elite English boarding school in a time not too distant from our own. It all seems perfectly normal but gradually from a few asides and the actions of some teachers, the reader begins to detect some troubling facts. It turns out that the students are destined to be donors, because they are clones for people who may need their organs. The true horror is not only that society by a calculus of crude utility countenances this practice, but also that the students are conditioned to never question their fate. As the young donor, Ruth, admits to her friends, "I was pretty much ready when I became a donor. It felt right. After all, it's what we're supposed to be doing."[44]

The novelist Margaret Atwood takes the transhuman possibility to another level in *Oryx and Crake*. The central character, Jimmy, lives in a post-apocalyptic landscape. We gradually realize in his musings that he had lived in a very technologically advanced world. In the pre-apocalyptic world, there was a biotechnical revolution in which companies maximized profits by controlling people's lives and environments. The employees affiliated with these companies lived in guarded compounds where they experienced drug induced raptures, perpetual youth, and lived off bioengineered plants and animals that maximized food production. Jimmy's friend, Crake, had bioengineered in his enclosed lab called Paradice a new species of "Crakers" that are passive leaf eaters who only have sex to procreate. In order to save a decaying human society, Crake creates an agent that produces a pandemic that is disguised and distributed as a prophylactic that kills off most humans except Jimmy, who has been immunized. The new world belongs to the Crakers although Jimmy becomes their guide. In their post-apocalyptic Eden, the Crakers begin

---

43. Warren, et al., "Highly Efficient Reprogramming," 1–13.

44. Ishiguro, *Never Let Me Go*, 227.

to probe religious questions of origins and meaning. Atwood's novel is a highly effective cautionary tale about the danger of having the ultimate power to transform our environment. It also warns us of the risks from turning technical capabilities into idols beyond questioning or reproach.

Such literary allies, as Merton recognized in his own time, can provide a compelling narrative of the negative consequences of adopting certain technologies in the future. They can effectively question in their fiction the utilitarian assumptions and distorted utopian aspirations of transhumanism. With such allies and Merton's principles, we can thoughtfully challenge transhumanism's desire to perfect humanity.

The distorted desire for cloning and prolonging life are examples of a materialism that radically manipulates creation. At its root the problem is that such a materialist vision is incapable of understanding human life in its totality, in both its sensible and spiritual aspects. For Merton this cramped vision of a technical mentality needs to be reshaped by a Christian humanism that expands the horizon of human life. In support of this objective, Merton discovered in theoria physike an applicable approach to nature that combined the sensible and spiritual. The mistake of those who advance certain technologies is that they are limited in their vision; they manipulate nature for the purposes of human utility. The impulse to explore the sensible is not wrong per se, but it is mistaken if it does not encompass a broader vision, one that includes a search for a divine purpose, the ultimate telos of the material world. This was why Merton believed the evolutionary theologian Pierre Teilhard de Chardin was so important, because he recognized the role of material and spiritual energies transforming life as part of a divine plan. Without sacrificing scientific objectivity or technological utility, Teilhard reintroduced the divine role and purpose in propelling physical creation back to its source and origin. With a good creation that is central to salvation, a Christian cannot approach nature indifferently but approaches it with respect, caution, and a sensibility for the deeper patterns and purposes inherent in creation.[45]

Hence, technology must be placed in the service of our humanity so that members of a just community can pursue their "total vocation" as human beings.[46] Merton realizes that there is much at stake in our choices. Do we have the wisdom to make the right judgments? He warns

---

45. Merton, *An Introduction to Christian Mysticism*, 124–31.
46. Merton, "Technology," 55–57.

that, "It would be a tragedy, when so much good has been accomplished and when so much can really be done with the amazing power of science, if the whole thing were to run away with us . . . Unfortunately the lack of balance between technology and spiritual life is so enormous that there is every chance of failure and accident . . ."[47]

47. Merton, *WF*, 232. "Letter to Elbert R. Sisson" (February-March, 1962).

CHAPTER 5

Some Balm for Gilead

Is there no balm in Gilead? Is there no physician there?

Jeremiah 8:22

Wisdom is radiant and unfading, and she is easily discerned by those who love her, and is found by those who seek her. She hastens to make herself known to those who desire her. He who rises early to seek her will have no difficulty, for he will find her sitting at his gates. To fix one's thought on her is perfect understanding, and he who is vigilant on her account will soon be free from care, because she goes about seeking those worthy of her, and she graciously appears to them in their paths, and meets them in every thought.

Wisdom 6:12–16

The Paradox of Technology

HUMANITY FINDS ITSELF IN a quandary, a paradox. The products of the technological world offer us amazing powers to assist our lives. There are even more astonishing possibilities on the horizon. This should be good news, and yet we may not be convinced that we now live or will soon live in the best of all possible worlds. And technology is not only part of the solution but also part of the problem. The threat of annihilation from weapons of mass destruction still looms. In our personal lives, we suffer from the frenzied pace of a communication overload. We wonder, according to the theologian Colin Gunton, how "a world dedicated to the pursuit of leisure and of machines that save labor is chiefly marked by its levels of rush, frenetic busyness and stress."[1] New biotechnologies offer a mixed blessing, the benefit of healing medical treatments and the dangerous temptation to perfect the human species.

But turning to the here and now, how do we pursue our daily lives in this technological world? In high school I served on the student council. We loved to bring our principal, Bob Chambers, a list of complaints. He often responded by asking our role in solving the problems. This tactic was aggravating, but he had a point. It is easier to criticize than to offer solutions. Having presented Merton's criticisms, I feel obliged to present some hopeful possibilities for engaging the technological world today. Merton's wisdom is not only prophetic; it also offers positive options for humanizing our technological world.

Any positive engagement must begin with a mental transformation in each of us as we seek to become thoughtful and spiritual persons who can contribute to true communities. Merton stated that we should begin by "learning to admit values, which we fear, from which we are trying to escape. Values like solitude, inner silence, reflective communion with natural realities, simple and genuine affection for other people, admission of our need for contemplation . . . Naturally, there is much more involved than this: but this might be a conceivable point of departure, a preparation for the recovery of freedom."[2] Moreover, one of Merton's lessons that I have discussed in previous chapters was the need to have a vital religious life through liturgy, prayer, deep reading, and careful reflection.

Seeking A Balanced Form of Work

If we want to fully integrate these contemplative values into our technological world, work is a good place to start. We spend countless hours working, on average around 1800 hours per adult each year in the United States.[3] Given these long hours, perhaps we should not be surprised that work can be a substitute form of religion with its immense seriousness

1. Johnson, "How Shall We Then Rest?"

2. Merton, *CGB*, 332.

3. Fleck, "International Comparison of Hours Worked."

and rituals. The human being as worker is too often secondary to the needs of the economic system. The inescapable force of this reality was palpable to Merton when he dropped off a package at a General Electric factory in Louisville. He confessed that the "religious seriousness of the monastery is like sandlot baseball compared with the big-league seriousness of General Electric."[4]

This Louisville plant represented the embodiment of the productive mentality that had been exhibited in an alternative form in the monastery for many years. The problem was not work per se. Gainful employment was not inherently good or evil, but must be judged by the extent to which it promoted the contemplative life. Moderate amounts of labor could "purify and pacify the mind and dispose [a person] for contemplation." The recovery of a balanced approach to work must assume a correct anthropology, a balanced understanding of the ends of human life. Adam was placed in the garden to "till it and keep it" but this labor was consonant with maintaining a "union with God," a "contact with all reality at its source."[5] In his own day Merton remarked that moderate work is a good but "the work men do because they are driven by ambition or love of money is quite another thing. They may 'like' it, but it is nevertheless slavery. Its orientation is exactly the opposite of the one we are considering here. Adam's work was worship. The work of those who work because they are driven by passion or cupidity is not worship but struggle, not freedom but (psychologically) compulsion."[6]

Excessive labor may be required to provide a person their sustenance, but it did not constitute a fitting employment. Using an employee like a tool can become a form of oppression in which the laborer lives merely to work instead of working to live. Efficiency further destabilizes family and community life. For example, constant employee relocations proceed regardless of the consequences to a family or community.[7]

The technological mentality of our age nurtures a hyper-productive mentality in our age of global competitiveness. Bill Gates is the poster boy for this mentality that is opposed to a contemplative conception of time. He once said of religion, "just in terms of allocation of time resources, religion is not very efficient. There's a lot more I could be doing on a

4. Merton, *CGB*, 232.

5. Merton, *The New Man*, 79–80.

6. Ibid.

7. Merton, "The Christian in a Technological World."

Saturday morning."[8] This honest admission by Gates reflects his desire for measurable productivity. Who can blame him? Gates demands tangible results—new products, greater market share, and higher profits. What could a religious service possibly give him: two units of grace in exchange for two units of prayer? Merton abhorred such a mentality of productivity, a mentality that had at times even infected his own monastery, as when the monks ran out to their fields like a football team entering a stadium.[9]

Instead, modern forms of production should humanely seek to facilitate the reintegration of the person, body, and soul. Merton observed that reintegration required a new mental framework in which work was done at a humane pace and for a limited number of hours a day. Such work would provide the kind of mental peace essential to connecting with God.[10] We know things are balanced when "everything is in unity, in order, at peace. Work no longer interferes with prayer or prayer with work. Contemplation no longer needs to be a special 'state' that removes one from the ordinary things going on around him for God penetrates all."[11]

How to Use Technology Instead of It Using You

The problems Merton detected in the work offered by industrial systems demonstrated the hegemony of Ellul's "technique." The products of such systems promoted a false belief in human control although they could at times present spiritual opportunities. An airplane that passed from Florida to Chicago over the monastery was a symbol of our false sense of controlling nature. Contemplation, unlike the flight to Chicago, "suspends modern life" and truly "gets you somewhere."[12] Of course, Merton would later desire to be on such planes to fly to conferences. Despite this desire he recognized that the millions traveling in airplanes were not necessarily going anywhere so "perhaps going nowhere is better."[13] The

8. Isaacson, "In Search of the Real Bill Gates."

9. Merton, "Answers for Hernan Lavin Cerda," 6; Merton, *The School of Charity*, 68–69, "Letter to Dom Gregorio Lemercier" (October 23, 1953).

10. Merton, *No Man Is an Island*, 109.

11. Merton, *Thoughts in Solitude*, 84–85.

12. Cunningham, *Spiritual Master*, 215.

13. Merton, *LL*, 266, entry of July 18, 1967.

rapidity of modern travel could also disrupt a sense of proportion and continuity. On one round trip flight, Merton was disoriented from leaving Gethsemani and returning home in less than forty-eight hours. This form of travel prompted an intense desire to purge "the violence of that one day's journey."[14]

Despite such criticisms, air travel could be a source of reflection on immanence and transcendence. On his final Asian journey, he described the take-off from San Francisco as "ecstatic."[15] A flight from Indianapolis to Minnesota in 1956 inspired a poem, "White Pasture." The airplane suspended the passenger between heaven and earth. He meditated on the eternal possibilities among the clouds. Yet, the serving of a meal was a reminder to "do something Earthy lest we become too spiritual." He was suspended between an "Elysium of upper air" and "the food of earth so graced with all that is true." The possibility for such meditations remained "unremarked, unlooked at" by most of the passengers who were numbed by their modern preoccupations. They continued to "go nowhere."[16]

The automobile, as a part of a noisy and relentless ground transportation system, had negative implications for a fully human life. It wasted resources, clogged streets, and was symptomatic of a mythic American "flight from reality." As Merton listened to cars pass on the highway not far from the abbey, he noted the "alien frenzy" of their "madly going somewhere for no reason."[17] The car was a fitting symbol for understanding the compulsions of a technological culture because "the attachment of the modern American to his automobile and the *symbolic* role played by his car, with its aggressive and lubric design, its useless power, its otiose gadgetry, its consumption of fuel, which is advertised as having almost supernatural power . . . that is where the study of American mythology should begin."[18]

The car also represented a thoughtless reality where the concern of automobile makers was to promote speed, fashion, and status in order to boost sales, not safety. Merton cited Ralph Nader's battles with the automobile industry to make cars safer as an example of how the automobile

14. Merton, *SS*, 3, entry of July 25, 1952.

15. Merton, *The Asian Journals*, 4.

16. Merton, *SS*, 53–54, entry of July 22, 1956. Merton wrote during another flight in 1956 that, "if you can be quiet in a plane it is a wonderful place in which to meditate." Merton, *SS*, 62, entry of August 4, 1956.

17. Merton, *LL*, 316, entry of June 18, 1966.

18. Merton, *CGB*, 76. Merton never learned to drive himself.

industry was indifferent to safety concerns. In that case ethics deferred to profitability.[19] Merton encountered another instrument of idolatry promoted by a different sort of disorder. Television was becoming a mainstay of American culture during his life. In 1962, polls estimated that 90 percent of households had a television and the average viewing period was several hours per day.[20] Although he had never seen an extended amount of television, friends informed him of its basic features. Merton believed that these long viewing hours promoted a numbing passivity instead of a religious awareness with its "ascent to a supremely active passivity in understanding and love."[21] America was rapidly "becoming a society of open mouthed and passive TV watchers."[22] This passivity rendered an individual susceptible to any illusory image on the screen.[23] In a letter to the Polish writer, Czelaw Milosz, Merton lamented that, "the poison is exactly the alienation you speak of, and it is not the individual, not society, but what comes of being an individual helpless to liberate himself from the images that society fills him with. It is a very fine picture of hell sometimes. When I see advertisements I want to curse they make me so sick and I do curse them."[24] The escape from this stream of visual nonsense must begin with turning off the television and engaging in "serious reading" and "articulate discussion."[25]

Small-scale technological inventions could raise parallel concerns, although they could also nurture aesthetic and contemplative experiences. The camera provided an example of the evolution of Merton's thoughts on smaller technologies. He confessed to being "terribly camera shy" in 1961. He decried "the awful instantaneous snapshot of pose, of falsity eternalized."[26] The camera could also intrude on his privacy. Visitors to Gethsemani often wanted to preserve a piece of him by photographing the famous monk during his reflections.[27]

---

19. Merton, "Marxism and Technology" in Dekar, *Thomas Merton*, 217.

20. Merton, *TTW*, 259, entry of October 22, 1962.

21. Merton, *New Seeds of Contemplation*, 86.

22. Merton, *HGB*, 316, "Letter to Erich Fromm" (September 26, 1961).

23. Merton, *CT*, 48, "Letter to Jacques Maritain" (March 7, 1966).

24. Merton, *CT*, 72, "Letter to Czelaw Milosz" (March 28,1961).

25. Merton, *WF*,169, "Letter to Mr. L. Dickson" (September 12, 1965).

26. Merton, *TTW*, 180, entry of November 17, 1961.

27. Merton, *ES*, 32, 38, 232, entries of (December 14, 1946), (February 1, 1947), (September 9, 1948).

Many years later, however, his views would change dramatically. Fascinated by the photographs of John Howard Griffin, Merton borrowed his camera as early as 1964 and became a proficient photographer. He was thus initiated into his "love affair" with the camera.[28] Griffin loaned him a camera in 1968 that he gratefully employed in the months before his death. The terms for his acceptance of the camera were instructive. Griffin could have it back at any time including his death. The camera must not be coveted; its purpose was not profit or status but to provide an artistic lens.[29] He had learned that "the camera does not know what it takes: it captures materials with which you reconstruct not so much what you saw as what you thought you saw. Hence photography is aware, mindful, of illusion and uses illusion, permitting and encouraging it—especially unconscious and powerful illusions that are not normally admitted on the scene."[30]

On his many walks he photographed whatever came across his path, particularly the random object, placed where their creator left it. The camera in these instances became a "catalyst for contemplation." It created mental images and a "heightened awareness very similar to meditative prayer."[31] The camera was an instructive example of how a machine could assist the contemplative life. Other machines offered contemplative opportunities. The record player at the hermitage provided a source of art in the form of music. Merton mastered a tape recorder that he received in 1967. It allowed him to record his thoughts in an oral form where he could be more open in his style. This openness was perfectly congruous with Merton's rejection of simplistic and static formulas in regard to contemplative thought.[32]

The use of small-scale technologies to enhance the contemplative life invoked a spirit of reasonable accommodation to the modern world consistent with his religious vocation. He also learned from the Shakers, who

28. Merton, *DWL*, 149, entry of September 26, 1964.

29. Mott, *The Seven Mountains of Thomas Merton*, 409, 461, 471, 481, 516. This interest in photography stood in marked contrast to Merton's boredom with photography in 1939 when he visited a Museum of Modern Art exhibit of Charles Scheeler. The photographs were "neat and so precise and so completely uninteresting." Merton, *Run to the Mountain*, 68.

30. Merton, *The Asian Journals*, 153.

31. Hart, "Photography and Prayer in Thomas Merton," 2–5; Griffin, *A Hidden Wholeness*, 49.

32. Mott, *The Seven Mountains of Thomas Merton*, 481.

had developed a proper understanding of craft technology. The Shakers were a Christian sect that had broken with the Quakers and believed in celibacy, universal brotherhood, pacifism, and the equality of the sexes. They shared their goods in communal living. Theologically, they believed that their founder, Mother Anne, was the reincarnation of Christ. They accepted the paradise myth of America. Their crafts reflected this unique American vision.[33]

Merton observed the purity of Shaker crafts in a visit to a former colony near the monastery. The buildings and furniture were pure testimonies to faith that provided a counterpoint to Western technology. They were simple, yet warm, visionary but sane. Their crafts were not done for an anonymous consumer in massive quantities, but to support communal values.[34] The Shakers attuned their artisanship with the spirit of creation, a divine presence operating through the ecology of the land, the potential of the wood, and the intended use of the object. As a result, their tables and chairs exhibit a "highly mystical quality, capaciousness, dignity, solidity, permanence."[35] Merton hoped that similar crafts might be developed in the monastery. After photographing a number of old baskets, Merton sought unsuccessfully to revive interest in the abbey's forgotten craft of basket weaving. This craft had fallen into disuse because of the profitability of cheese.[36]

The camera, the tape recorder, and craft skills exhibited technical methods and capacities consistent with a contemplative life. These benefits prompted an admission by Merton in 1967 that he might need to "take back some of the things that I have said about technology."[37] When there was a misapplication of technology, the machine was often an innocent, a medium through which human errors were transmitted and magnified. By learning how to make prudential judgments by using contemplative principles, humanity could learn how to assess and properly use technologies.

33. Fluornoy, "Thomas Merton and the Shakers," 7–8; Merton, WF, 30–31, "Letter to Mary Childs Black" (January 24, 1962).

34. Merton, "Introduction," vii–xv; Merton, "The Shakers," 37–41; Merton, HGL, 36–37, "Letter to Edward Deming Andrews" (December 21, 1961); Merton, HGL, 40, "Letter To Mrs. Edward Deming Andrews" (July 20, 1964).

35. Merton, An Introduction to Christian Mysticism, 133–34.

36. "Merton and Basket Weaving," 10.

37. Mott, The Seven Mountains of Thomas Merton, 481.

Creation's Healing Power: Restoration in Nature

While large or smaller scale technologies provided both challenges and opportunities to the contemplative life, Merton knew that nature could heal many of the wounds of the technological world. Through nature, we learn that there "is an unspeakable secret: paradise is all around us and we do not understand. It is wide open . . . but we do not know it: we are off 'one to his farm and another to his merchandise.' Lights on. Clocks ticking. Thermostats working. Stoves cooking. Electric shavers filling radios with static. 'Wisdom,' cries the dawn deacon, but we do not attend."[38]

So, we must return to nature and learn its lessons. Merton only had to gaze into the Kentucky night sky to be reminded of the divine. In its etymological roots, contemplation meant to look for portents in a portion of the sky. Merton loved this connection. He had shown an interest in stars since childhood when he learned about them from his grandmother. As a college student, he had taken a course on astronomy at Columbia.[39] With this background, it was not surprising that he opened his autobiography, *Seven Story Mountain*, with an astrological reference. "On the last day of 1915, under the sign of the Water Bearer, in a year of a great war, and down in the shadow of some French mountains on the borders of Spain, I came into the world."[40]

These reflections and many others by Merton stood in contrast to a technological world in which nature was being constantly manipulated. Creation was more than a resource. This was the lesson previously discussed of theoria physike; nature revealed the mystery of the divine presence that operated in and through matter.[41] Nature could restore spiritual health because it was "a blind sweet point" where sapiential wisdom could "collect and manifest itself."[42]

> There is in all visible things an invisible fecundity, a dimmed light, a meek namelessness, a hidden whole-ness. This mysterious Unity and Integrity is Wisdom, the Mother of all, *Natura naturans*. There is in all things an inexhaustible sweetness and purity, a silence that is a fount of action and joy. It rises up in word-less gentleness and flows out to me from the unseen roots

38. Merton, *CGB*, 132.
39. Mott, *The Seven Mountains of Thomas Merton*, 108.
40. Merton, *The Seven Story Mountain*, 7.
41. Merton, *An Introduction to Christian Mysticism*, 126–31.
42. Merton, *CGB*, 131.

of all created being, welcoming me tenderly, saluting me with
indescribable humility. This is at once my own being, my own
nature, and the Gift of my Creator's Thought and Art within me,
speaking as Hagia Sophia, speaking as my sister, Wisdom.[43]

Unfortunately, human pride could ignore this integrating wisdom. To il-
lustrate this point Merton fashioned a modern myth relying on ancient
typologies and characters. He had loved myths since his school days and
they provided "coherent models of experience" in contrast to the frac-
tured perspectives of modern life. In "Atlas and the Fatman," the myth
had three main characters. There was the Titan, Atlas, who represented
the forces of nature; there was the deluded Fat Man, representing modern
man, who wished to be an all-powerful deity; and there was the sympa-
thetic narrator. On his journey in the world, the narrator observed the Fat
Man attempting to command nature. He was the symbol of a technological society that attempted to dominate its environment. By contrast, Atlas
was a symbol of nature that represented the potential for spontaneous
order and beauty. Atlas was a representative of natural forces that desired
reconciliation with humanity. If there were an appropriate response from
humanity, Atlas would reciprocate by providing mankind with peace and
wholeness.[44]

This myth suggested how the gift of nature, of God's creation, had
been either ignored or abused in American culture. A failure to respect
nature was often the consequence of a domination mentality, a ceaseless
quest for control that precipitated violence and destruction. For example,
the male "virility cult," as exemplified by the writer Ernest Hemingway,
exploited nature at every turn.[45] The Puritans despised the "hideous and
desolate wilderness" that represented sinister forces and an uncontrolled
domain of moral wickedness. The spontaneity of nature spawned sin. The
reward for taming this dark realm was prosperity.[46]

Fortunately, the Transcendentalists proposed an alternative inter-
pretation that opposed neither the paradise or wicked wilderness inter-
pretations. The Transcendentalists were a nineteenth-century American
literary movement who believed in the spiritual intuition of the individual

43. Merton, "Hagia Sophia," in Merton, *The Collected Poems of Thomas Merton*,
363.

44. Merton, *RU*, 91–111.

45. Merton, "Elegy for Ernest Hemingway," 37–38.

46. Merton, *Day of a Stranger*, 17.

that could transcend science and religious traditions. Nature was for the Transcendentalists the realm of God, a location for healing and sanity. It offered a psychological component of irrationality, spontaneity, and impulse to balance the excesses of an unchecked rationalism in the city. In addition to the Transcendentalists, Merton borrowed from the naturalist, John Muir, who believed that humanity yearned for a wild place where God could be heard. Here, animals can be viewed in terms of kinship in the midst of an "unchanged natural existence." All creatures had the right to exist on their own terms because of a fundamental respect for life.[47]

The woods of Gethsemani were also a place of mental and spiritual renewal. Here Merton was freed of the perpetual movement and noise of the abbey; there were ample opportunities for waiting, watching, and listening. The experience of simple realities like pools of water, the singing of frogs or leafless trees witnessed to the mercy and fecundity of God. Borrowing from the Jesuit poet Gerard Manley Hopkins, he noted how each animal and flower had an "inscape," a unified composition of unique features that was their "sanctity."[48]

Providing an important lesson for the communication age, recent psychological studies have shown that spending time in nature sharpens our attention and improves our memory and cognition. The reason, according to attention restoration theory, is that people calm their working memory and use their higher cognitive faculties when they are not flooded by external stimuli. A calm mind can think more cogently and has better access to higher emotions such as empathy and compassion.[49]

Merton was well aware of the emotional and cognitive benefits of his time in the woods. In many of his most trying moments, nature became a resource for centering a life dangerously close to spinning out of control. On one troubled evening in 1966 he reported that, "tonight walked up and down on the cool, clear evening, in the full moon, meditating, enjoying the quiet, the peace, the cool silence of the valley, and the freedom.

47. Merton, "The Wild Places," 95–107. Merton acknowledged that many of his ideas on wilderness are taken from Nash, *Wilderness and the American Mind*; Merton, "Wilderness and Paradise," 83–89. He was taught by two Thoreau scholars at Columbia, Joseph Wood Krutch and Mark Van Doren. Merton, *WF*, 71, "Letter to Harry J. Cargas" (February 14, 1966); Merton, *RJ*, 222, "Letter to Sister Therese Lentfoehr" (September 25, 1956).

48. Merton, *New Seeds of Contemplation*, 14, 30.

49. Berman, et al., "The Cognitive Benefits of Interacting with Nature," 1207–12; Immordino-Yang, et al., "Neural Correlates of Admiration and Compassion," 8021–26.

All I have ever sought is here: how foolish not to be content with it—and let anything trouble it, without need."[50]

Nature was a realm of self-contained balance, a point of contrast to the technological cycle of production and consumption. A person could be both participant and observer here without having to achieve any goals or produce any results. The sense of connection between nature and a divine creation was heightened by life at the hermitage.

> Today was *the* prophetic day, the first of the real shining Spring . . . Freezing night, but cold bright morning, and a brave, bright shining of sun that is new, and an awakening in all the land as if the earth was aware of its capacities! . . . The morning got more and more brilliant and I could feel the brilliancy of it get- ting into my own blood. Living so close to the cold, you feel the spring. And this is man's mission! The earth cannot *feel* all this. We must. But living away from the earth and the trees we fail them. We are absent from the wedding feast.[51]

The gifts of nature to humanity invited a reciprocal gift of ecological sensitivity. This sensitivity was often blocked in the modern world by a "technocratic and self-centered 'worldliness' " in which we judge "every- thing in relation to [ourselves]."[52] The goal should instead be an "eco- logical balance" because the modern world had the capacity to destroy the creation. Merton was alarmed by Rachel Carson's book *Silent Spring*, which asserted that technology's constant imperative for efficiency had promoted the use of insecticides that threatened the environment.[53]

While Merton recognized the dangers of our manipulating the en- vironment, the idea of tending nature as a garden could also be a posi- tive model. There were biblical precedents. For example, Adam had been placed in a garden to "till it and keep it." Adam was thus "from the start" to "act as God's instrument in cultivating and developing the natural creation."[54] Here, the work of the human being in cooperation with God was essential. Nature in this context preserved a sense of humility and piety that has been lost in the technological society. In exchange for the many gifts of nature, there was a duty of stewardship, a gentle dominion.

50. Merton, *LL*, 151, entry of October 27, 1966.

51. Ibid., 18–19, entry of February 17, 1966.

52. Merton, *CGB*, 294.

53. Merton, *The School of Charity*, 27–28, "Letter to Abbot James Fox" (October 7, 1951); Merton, *HGL*, 213–14, "Letter to W.H. Ferry" (January 12, 1963).

54. Merton, *The New Man*, 78.

God had the authority to revoke this stewardship if we abused his trust as he did in the case of Eden.[55]

A Philosophy of Solitude

A proper balance of work and life, a preference for small-scale technologies, and restoration in nature allowed us to begin to reintegrate our humanity and build balanced communities. For Merton all of these efforts were grounded in a philosophy of solitude. A fundamental assumption of this philosophy was the falsity created by endless technological diversions and temptations. Beneath this falsity, a contemplative discovered "an abyss of irrationality, confusion, pointlessness, and indeed of apparent chaos."[56]

The solitary life did not reject their society, they must "transcend" their society. This was possible if we reintegrated ourselves by seeking a "spiritual and simple oneness" in ourselves. This oneness allowed for a connection to all other people in a form of solidarity that rejected the ·special interests and ideals of a narrow group. Unlike the collective delusions of modern society, this unity was connection on a "deeper and mystical level" that pursued a purity of love. How do we know that we were pursuing a life of balanced solitude? Behind the outer complexity, there was a life of simplicity marked by candor, gentleness, and deep sympathy. This life of simplicity avoided forms of the Christian faith that were too complicated in their visible and social dimension.[57]

This life presumed the need to communicate prophetic messages and God's mercy, but was leery about how to proceed. For Merton, silence was part of the answer. It was certainly required to proclaim the truths of God and to experience the divine.

> The message of God's mercy to man must be preached. The word of truth must be proclaimed. No one can deny this. But there are not a few who are beginning to feel the futility of adding more words to the constant flood of language that pours meaninglessly over everybody, everywhere, from morning to night. For language to have meaning there must be intervals of silence somewhere, to divide word from word and utterance

55. Merton, *HGL*, 506, "Letter to Rosemary Radford Ruether" (March 19, 1967).
56. Merton, *DQ*, 177–79.
57. Ibid., 179–89.

> from utterance. He who retires into silence does not necessarily hate language. Perhaps it is love and respect for language, which imposes silence upon him. For the mercy of God is not heard in words unless it is heard, both before and after the words are spoken, in silence.[58]

So we pursued a life of silence in order to reintegrate our true selves freed from the "illusions and facades" of the world. In our true self we experience a peace that facilitated our connection to God and other human beings from a position of charity. This was the calling of the solitary.[59]

Although he candidly outlined many problems with technology, Merton believed we could restore our true selves amidst the diminishments of the technological world. The restoration would include sane forms of work, appropriate small-scale technologies, the encouraging of crafts, a tapping into the restorative possibilities of nature, and learning the lessons of the solitary. If we pursued these possibilities with wisdom, we could recover our connection to a divine reality and promote a new balance in our lives. This balance was what Merton defined as a form of "mental ecology" where the contemplative was attuned to the full presence of life. And what would such a full life contain? In one of his journals, he records how he experienced one morning the "symphony of existence" that blended the sound of birds singing, the smell of black coffee in the morning, and the reading of the Chinese philosopher, Chuang Tzu.[60]

58. Ibid., 194–95.
59. Ibid., 192–95.
60. Merton, *DWL*, 239–40, entry of May 1965.

Conclusion
From the Watchtower

I shall stand at my post, I shall station myself on my Watchtower, watching to see what he will say to me . . .

Habakkuk 2:1

Further points:

Among the special problems that might be kept in mind, we might consider the nature of the technological society, whether such a society is by its very nature oriented to self-destruction, or whether it can on the contrary be regarded as a source of hope for a new sacral order, a millennial "city" in which God will be manifested and praised in the freedom and enlightenment of man . . .

Thomas Merton,
"Notes from Retreat of November 1964: Spiritual Roots of Protest"

The Choice

THOMAS MERTON STATED HIS abilities to contribute an analysis of the modern world as follows,

The contemplative will, then, concern himself with the same problems as other people but he will try to get to the spiritual and metaphysical roots of these problems . . . I cannot clam that I have discovered anything worth saying. Yet since I have been asked to say something, I will at least hazard a few conjectures. Take them for what they may be worth: they are subjective, they

are provisional, they are mere intuitions, they will certainly need
to be completed by the thinking of others. If they suggest a few
useful perspectives to others, I will be satisfied.[1]

We learn two things from this statement. Merton will seek the spiritual
and metaphysical roots of our technological problems. He also claimed
a limited analysis. As for the second claim, Merton, despite his alleged
limitations, had profound insights about technology and these insights
were much more than a few conjectures or mere intuitions. To para-
phrase Shakespeare, methinks he doth protest too much. Indeed, Merton
provided us with an invaluable framework for clearing away the weeds of
our modern technological culture in order to focus on our ultimate destiny, "the hidden wholeness" that was our foundation as people of God.
The "purity of heart" of the Desert Fathers, the theoria physike of Saint
Maximus, and the philosophy of the solitary guide us towards this reality. These contemplative foundations were nurtured by both an internal
spiritual quest and the benefits of a free and loving community. These
foundations were different in their focus and content, but they all aspired
to that ultimate form of wisdom, sapientia, that united then transcended
both reason and intuition, the solitary and the community, in order to
enlighten the quest for the ultimate reality.

But there was a threat to this spiritual quest. A technological mentality had been insinuating itself into our consciousness. Without being
aware of it, we allowed a mentality of efficiency and productivity to become our highest priorities. As a result the assumptions and compulsions of technique replaced a deep discernment in faith. We created new
technical powers and then applied them without thinking about the consequences. Hence, we have risked massively destructive wars, adopted
mind-numbing information technologies, and may, in the near future,
try to perfect ourselves through a host of new biotechnologies. This collective society fostered an excessive focus on relentless work, mental passivity, and the exclusion of spiritual values in order to achieve its ends.
As a result of our choices, we craved consumer goods, scientific achieve-
ments, and mindless forms of sensation. Despite these problems, there
were solutions such as a work/life balance, learning how to properly use
technologies, and applying the restorative powers of nature.

If we turn to religion as an antidote, we must be careful. The technological mentality can be present here as well. When I was practicing

1. Merton, FV, 147.

law years ago, I went on a silent retreat for a week. During the retreat, I still wanted to schedule my spiritual life. Having lived my work life in billable increments, I created a detailed list of activities and their scheduled times for each day that included reading, prayer, religious services, and walking. I yearned for constant structure and activity, because I was pressing to ward off the silence. My objective was also to improve my spiritual productivity. I would leverage my spiritual assets and obtain an optimal effect. And of course I did not. As my experience suggests, the spirit of productivity, formulas, and efficiency that are endemic to the world of technology can enter anywhere, including the spiritual life. Merton warned about people like me on that retreat who seek to "achieve contemplation as the fruit of planned effort and of spiritual ambition. He will assume varied attitudes, meditate on the inner significance of his own postures, and try to fabricate for himself a contemplative identity: and all the while there is nobody there. There is only an illusory, fictional 'I' which seeks itself, struggles to create itself out of nothing, maintained in being by its own compulsion and the prisoner of his own private illusion."[2]

Merton realized that the technological idols of modern life had infected even religion. Another symptom of this infection is that we may covet a kind of personal infallibility derived from our spiritual connection. All we have to do is be in with the "big Boss, the Chief upstairs in his office on the top floor of the Babel National Bank."[3] He will turn on the tap of enrichment from which will flow a big home, a perfect spouse, saintly children, and a low golf handicap. Moreover, we will receive perfect discernment, holiness, and the ability to guide others in our own image.

Given this and many other temptations of the current age, we will need all of the wisdom that Merton or anyone else can provide to navigate the waves of complexities and confusions roiling our technological world. We will always be confronted with choices: we can live on the surface of our technological culture passively accepting the continual diminishments of our humanity, or we can pierce this surface and "recover our inner faith not only in God but in the good in reality, and in the power of the good to take care of itself and us as well, if we only attend to it, observe, listen, choose and obey."[4] If we choose the path of

2. Merton, *The Inner Experience*, 5.
3. Ibid., 130.
4. Merton, *CGB*, 119.

contemplative wisdom, however, we must be prepared for its demands because "the solitary is one who is called to make one of the most terrible decisions possible to man: the decision to disagree completely with those who imagine that the call to diversion and self-deception is the voice of truth . . . He must renounce the blessing of every convenient illusion that absolves him from responsibility when he is untrue to his deepest self and to his inmost truth—the image of God in his own soul."[5]

If we pursue the contemplative option, we must have the courage to realign our priorities. While he would not eliminate technologies, Merton knew that they must be constrained within the goals and ideals of a fully human community. In this community we can develop a life in conformity with contemplative principles, including the primary task that was to seek "the presence of God *in this present life*, in the world, and in myself, and my task as Christian is to live in full and vital awareness of this ground of my being and the world's being." Each person must also have "profound and solid grounding in spiritual principles, one must have a deep and persevering moral strength, a compassion, an attachment to truth and humanity, a faith in God, an uncompromising fidelity to God's law of love."[6] Merton noted that our "religious life including prayer, contemplation, and liturgy would help us to Acts and forms of worship [that] help one to do this, and the Church with her liturgy and sacraments, gives us the essential means of grace . . ."[7] Certainly prayer was a key aspect of this point for Merton. For example, certain meditative practices like lectio divina could pacify the frantic buzz of our communications overloaded minds and redirect our thoughts to the divine.

Merton knew that we must also change other aspects of our lives to reverse the negative impacts of an excessive devotion to a technological world. He posited certain guidelines for nurturing a contemplative life.

- Work enough to take care of your needs but consider that money should not be the primary consideration of your work. Consider a vow of modest living.

- Value in each day some quiet moments. This could include the early hours of the morning. This is the time of "new life, new beginning, and therefore important for the spiritual life." Consider going to early Mass.

5. Merton, *DQ*, 183.
6. Merton, *PCE*, 383.
7. Merton, *CGB*, 320.

- Find time to experience nature and the wonder of God's creation.

- Keep the Sabbath holy. This is a way to break into the "ceaseless, secular 'round' of time with a burst of light out of a sacred eternity." Our observance of Sunday reminds us of "*the peace that should filter through the whole week when our work is properly oriented.*"

- Pursue "active virtue and good works." We must faithfully fulfill our duties as parents, citizens, and members of a profession.

- "Penetrate the inner meaning of life in Christ and see the full significance of its demands . . . The virtue of a Christian is something creative and spiritual, not simply a fulfillment of a law."

- For married persons, the marriage should "bear witness to Christ's love for the world," for it is in marriage that we experience that love. It is a sign and an example of our desire for that ultimate unity and reality in God.[8]

In our quest for the wisdom to pursue these activities and many others in balancing our lives in a technological world, Merton's model suggested that we must seek allies among other faith traditions and even secular sources. For example, there is a national movement to adopt a simple, sustainable, and slow lifestyle. There is a National Vacation Matters Summit. A good example regarding a day of rest is the Jewish writer, Judith Shulevitz, who reminds us of the value of taking a day off in *The Sabbath World: Glimpses of a Different Order of Time*. She addresses our cultural ambivalence towards resting and reverence on a Sabbath in an efficiency-driven market society. She takes the plunge, decides to observe the Sabbath as a holy obligation, and realizes that such a commitment praises a creator greater than us. From our rest, we gain inner peace as well as a community spirit as we are "forced to turn towards one another." There is "rest time, recreational time, family time, time for friends and guests, and of course, time for God."[9]

Discovering Our Angels in a Machine World

Let me offer a final example of Merton's call to reintegration, holiness, and wisdom in a technological world. In 1967 for the magazine *Season*, a short-lived quarterly at the Dominican House of Studies at Berkeley,

8. Merton, *The Inner Experience*, 137–40.
9. Shulevitz, *The Sabbath World*, 37–38.

California, Merton explored the loss of the angelic presence in human life. The absence of the angels was part of the "death of God" phenomena, an inability to hear the heavenly messengers who were witnesses to the transcendent and arrived when human beings reached the limits of their natural strength and intelligence.

Angels were excluded from the modern world. They were "too dramatic and too mythical." Science had proven that they did not govern the stars as suggested by the teachings of the medieval saint, Thomas Aquinas, so they must not exist. Their presence was an unwanted reminder of human limitations. Unfortunately, their absence excluded a part of the personal dimension of divine revelation. The resulting domination of the abstractness of science robbed religion of grace, joy, and freedom.

In the modern world the machine was our messenger that provided information not the fullness of eternal being. We relied on technology for without technology urban life was impossible as was demonstrated by the New York blackout of 1965. In addition, the instruments of technology oriented us towards linear time instead of the eternal and serendipitous time of the heavenly host.[10]

Why was this change problematic? Behind the superficial harmony of the collectivity in a technological world, there was a "vast thoughtlessness." The angelic warnings and encouragements were replaced by the momentary, futile desires of production. The angels and their wisdom were exiles in our world and must be reclaimed at the frontiers, the boundaries of human experience. Despite the difficulty of our receiving them, we needed their presence "not to replace our machines but to teach us how to live with them. For the angels come to teach us how to rest, to forget useless care, to relax, in silence, to 'let go,' to abandon ourselves not in self-conscious fun but in self-forgetful faith . . . May they come back into our world and deliver it from its massive boredom, its metaphysical fatigue."[11]

Thus we return here to the heart of Merton's message on wisdom. Angels were our guide back to "self-forgetful faith" and thus to our connection with ultimate reality, God. If we have the wisdom to grant primacy to our engagement with the ultimate source of our reality, we can turn to our internal spiritual resources and deep wells of creativity, freedom, and spontaneity. As we turn inward, we can also turn externally with a fresh and vital vision that seeks to build true communities. We

10. St. Thomas Aquinas talks about a different kind of time with regard to angels: the "aevum." See *Summa Theologiae*, I.10.5.

11. Merton, "The Angel and the Machine," 3–6.

can do these things because we seek a God who "has sought us. God has come to take up His abode in us, in sinners. There is nothing further to look for except to turn to Him completely, where He is already present. Be quiet and see that he is God."[12]

12. Merton, *CGB*, 23.

Bibliography

Aboujouade, Elias. *Virtually You: The Dangerous Power of the E-Personality*. New York: Norton, 2011.

ACT. *Reading Between the Lines, What the ACT Reveals About College Readiness in Reading*. Online: http://www.act.org/research/policymakers/pdf/reading_report.pdf. 2006.

Ahrens, Frank. "The Acclerating Decline of Newspapers," *Washington Post* (October 27, 2009). Online: http://www.washingtonpost.com/wp-dyn/content/article/2009/10/26/AR2009102603272.html.

American Academy of Child and Adolescent Psychiatry. *Facts for Families*, No. 10 (May 2008). Online: http://www.aacap.org/galleries/FactsForFamilies/10_teen_suicide.pdf.

Anderholm, Judith. "Thomas Merton and Aldous Huxley." *The Merton Seasonal* 16 (Spring 1991) 8–10.

Andrews, Lori. *The Clone Age: Adventures in a New Age of Reproductive Technologies*. New York: Holt, 1999.

Arrison, Sonia. "Living to 100 and Beyond," *The Wall Street Journal* (August 27–28, 2011) C1, C2.

Arrison, Sonia. *100 Plus: How the Coming Age of Longevity Will Change Everything, From Careers and Relationships to Family and Faith*. New York: Basic, 2011.

Associated Press. "Scientist Creates Headless Frog Embryos in Laboratory," *Miami Herald* (October 17, 1997) 26A.

Audi, Tamara and Arlene Chang. "Assembling the Global Baby," *The Wall Street Journal* (December 11–12, 2010): C1.

Baker, Darren J., et al., "Clearance of p16ink4a_positive senescent cells delays ageing-associated disorders." (November 2, 2011). Online: http://www.nature.com/nature/journal/vaop/ncurrent/full/nature10600.htm.

Baron, Naomi S. *Always On: Language in an Online and Mobile World*. Oxford: Oxford University Press, 2008.

Bauerlein, Mark. *The Dumbest Generation*. New York: Tarcher, 2008.

Beauchamp, Tom and James Childress. *Principles of Biomedical Ethics*. 6th Edition. Oxford: Oxford University Press, 2008.

Berman, Mark G. et al., "The Cognitive Benefits of Interacting with Nature." *Psychological Science* 19 (December 2008) 1207–12.

Berman, Morris. *The Twilight of American Culture*. New York: Norton, 2000.

Bibliography

"The Best Way to Do Almost Anything on Your Mobile Devices." *The Wall Street Journal* (August 27, 2012), R 1.

Black Dog i-Tech Series. *iPhone & iPad: The Essentials*. 2011.

Boehret, Katherine. "Using Another Screen to Interact with the TV." *The Wall Street Journal* (December 21, 2011) D2.

Bunting, Madeline. *Willing Slaves: How the Overwork Culture is Ruling Our Lives*. New York: HarperCollins, 2004.

Bureau of Labor Statistics. "American Time Use Survey 2004–2008." Online: http://www.bls.gov/tus/.

Caplan, Arthur. "What's Morally Wrong with Eugenics?" In *Controlling Our Destinies*, edited by Philip R. Sloan, 209–23. Notre Dame: University of Notre Dame Press, 2000.

Carr, Nicholas. *The Shallows: What the Internet Is Doing to Our Brains*. New York: Norton, 2010.

Castranova, Edward. *Synthetic Worlds: The Business and Culture of Online Games*. Chicago: University of Chicago Press, 2005.

Changizi, Mark. "Masters of Distraction." *The Wall Street Journal* (August 20–21, 2011) C9.

Conley, Dalton. *Elsewhere U.S.A.* New York: Vintage, 2010.

Conze, Edward. *Buddhist Thought in India*. London: Allen and Unwin, 1962.

Crowell, Sheila E. "The Neurobiology of Declarative Memory." In *The Neurobiology of Learning: Perspectives from Second Language Acquisition*, edited by John H. Schumann, et al., 67–98. Mahwah, NJ: Erlbaum, 2004.

Cunningham, Lawrence. "The Monk as Critic of Culture." *The Merton Annual* 3 (1990) 189–97.

———. *Thomas Merton and the Monastic Vocation*. Grand Rapids: Eerdmans, 1999.

———. *Thomas Merton: Spiritual Master*. Mahwah, NJ: Paulist, 1992.

Daggy, Robert. "Choirs of Millions: A Reflection on Thomas Merton and God's Creatures." *Cistercian Studies Quarterly* 28 (1993) 93–107.

Daggy, Robert. "Introduction." In Thomas Merton, *Monks Pond*, ix–xvi. Lexington: University of Kentucky Press, 1989.

Davidson, Cathy N. *Now You See It*. New York: Viking, 2011.

Dawkins, Richard. "What's Wrong with Cloning?" In *Clones and Clones*, edited by Martha Nussbaum and Cass Sunstein, 54–66. New York: Norton, 1998.

de Grey, Aubrey. *Ending Aging: The Rejuvenation Breakthroughs that Could Reverse Human Aging in Our Lifetime*. New York: St. Martin's, 2007.

Deignan, Kathleen, SND. "The Forest Is My Bride" In Thomas Merton, *When the Trees Say Nothing*, 21–42. Notre Dame: Sorin, 2003.

Dekar, Paul R. *Thomas Merton: Twentieth-Century Wisdom for Twenty-First-Century Living*. Eugene, OR: Wipf and Stock, 2011.

———. "What the Machine Produces and What the Machine Destroys: Thomas Merton on Technology." *The Merton Annual* 17 (2004) 216–34.

Del Prete, Thomas. "On Mind, Matter and Knowing, Thomas Merton and Quantum Physics." In *The Vision of Thomas Merton*, edited by Patrick O'Connell and Patrick Hart, 119–33. Lexington, KY: University of Kentucky Press, 1989.

de Lubac, Henri. "Avant-Propos." In Pierre Teilhard de Chardin, *Lettres de Egypte 1905–1908*, 1–8. Aubier: Editions Montaigne, 1963.

———. *The Faith of Teilhard de Chardin*. London: Burns and Oates, 1964.

————. "Introduction." In Pierre Teilhard de Chardin, *Letters from Hastings*, 1–10. New York: Herder and Herder, 1968.

————. *The Religion of Teilhard de Chardin*. New York: Desclée, 1967.

————. "Teilhard de Chardin in the Context of Renewal." *Communio* 15:2 (Fall 1988) 361–75.

————. *Teilhard de Chardin: The Man and his Meaning*. New York: Hawthorn, 1965.

Dennett, Daniel. *Breaking the Spell: Religion as a Natural Phenomena*. New York: Viking, 2006.

Destefano, Diana and Jo-Anne LeFevre. "Cognitive Load in Hypertext Reading: A Review." *Computers in Human Behavior* 23 (May 2007) 1616–41.

de Zengotita, Thomas. *Mediated: How the Media Shapes Your World and the Way You Live in It*. New York: Bloomsbury, 2005.

Doctorow, Cory. "Writing in the Age of Distraction." *Locus* (January, 2009). Online: http://www.locusmag.com/Features/2009/01/cory-doctorow-writing-in-age-of.html.

Dolnick, Sam. "'Wombs for rent': The latest job outsourcing to India," *Atlanta Journal Constitution* (December 31, 2007) A7.

Dux, Paul E., et al., "Isolation of a Central Bottleneck of Information Processing with Time-Resolved fMRI1." *Neuron* 52 (December 21, 2006) 1109–20.

Elliot, Carl. *Better Than Well*. New York: Norton, 2004.

Elmore, Tim. *Generation iY: Our Last Chance to Save Their Future*. Atlanta: Poet Gardner, 2010.

Ernst and Young, "Biotech industry showing resilience despite challenging conditions." (April 28, 2010.) Online: http://www.ey.com/US/en/Newsroom/News-releases/Biotech-industry-showing-resilience-despite-challenging-conditions.

Farrell, James J. "Thomas Merton and the Religion of the Bomb." *Religion and American Culture* 5 (Winter 1995) 77–98.

Feenberg, Andrew. "Marcuse or Habermas: Two Critiques of Technology." *Inquiry* (1996) 45–70.

Fesquet, Henri. *The Drama of Vatican II*. New York: Random House, 1967.

Fleck, Susan. "International Comparison of Hours Worked: An Assessment of the Statistics." (2009.) Online: http://www.bls.gov/opub/mlr/2009/05/art1full.pdf.

Fluornoy, Judith. "Thomas Merton and the Shakers." *The Merton Seasonal* 22 (Spring 1997) 7–11.

Fowler, Geoffrey. "Facebook, One Billion and Counting." http://online.wsj.com/article/SB10000872396390443635404578036164027386112.html

Fowler, Geofffrey A. and Marie C. Baca. "The ABCs of E-Reading," *The Wall Street Journal* (August 25, 2010) D1, 2

Fukuyama, Francis. *Our Posthuman Future*. New York: Farrar, Straus & Giroux, 2001.

Galloway, Jim. "Delusions, The Legislature and an Implanted Microchip." (April 19, 2010.) Online: http:// blogs.ajc.com/political-insider-jim-galloway/2010/04/19/delusions-the-legislature-and-an-implanted-microchip/.

Georgia Senate Bill 230. "The Microchip Consent Act of 2010."

Gitlin, Todd. *Media Unlimited: How the Torrent of Images and Sounds Overwhelms Our World*. New York: Holt, 2002.

Glied, Sherry and Alison Evans Cuellar. "Trends And Issues In Child And Adolescent Mental Health Care." *Health Affairs* 22 (2003) 39–50.

Gnanayutham, Paul, et al. "Discrete Acceleration and Personalized Tiling as Brain-Body Inter-Face Paradigms for Neurorehabilitation." *CHI '05: Proceedings of the SIGCHI Conference on Human Factors in Computing Systems*, 261–70. New York: ACM Press, 2005.

Gould, Stephen J. *Rock of Ages*. Baltimore: Ballantine, 1999.

Greenblat, Alan. "Lawmakers Are Working on Anti-Brain-Chip Bill." (April 15, 2010.) Online: http://www.npr.org/blogs/alltechconsidered/2010/04/15/126023516/breathe-easy—ga—llawmakers-are-working-on-anti-brain-chip-bill.

Greenfield, Patricia M. "Technology and Informal Education: What is Taught, What is Learned?" *Science* 323 (January 2, 2009) 69–71.

Griffin, John Howard. *A Hidden Wholeness: The Visual World of Thomas Merton*. Boston: Houghton-Mifflin, 1970.

Grusser, S.M., et al. "Excessive computer game playing: evidence for addiction and aggression?" *Cyberspsychology and Behavior* 10 (April 2007): 290–92.

Grossman, Lev. "The Hyperconnected." *Time* (March 16, 2007.) Online: http://www.time.com/time/magazine/article/0,9171,1607260,00.html.

Hafner, Katie. "Texting May Be Taking a Toll on Teenagers," *New York Times* (May 25, 2009). Online: http://www.nytimes.com/2009/05/26/health/26teen.html.

Haier, R.J., et al. "Regional Glucose Metabolic Changes after Learning a Complex Visuospatial Motor Task: A Positron Emission Tomographic Study." *Brain Research* 570:1–2 (1992) 134–43.

Hamilton, Ryan, et al. "Being of two minds: Switching mindsets exhausts self-regulatory resources." *Organizational Behavior and Human Decision Processes* (2010.) Online: http:oi:10.1016/j.obhdp.2010.11.005.

Hammonds, Steve. "Impact of Internet Based Teaching on Student Achievement." *British Journal of Educational Technology* 34 (2003) 95–98.

Harmon, Amy. "Genetic Testing +Abortion=???" *New York Times* (May 13, 2007) sec. 4, 1, 4.

Hart, Betty and Todd R. Risley. *Meaningful Differences in the Everyday Experience of Young American Children*. Baltimore: Brookes, 1995.

Hart, Patrick, OCSO. "Photography and Prayer in Thomas Merton." *The Merton Seasonal* (Autumn 1985) 2–5.

Hartford, James. *Merton and Friends*. New York: Continuum, 2006.

Higgins, Michael. "Monasticism as Rebellion: The Blakean roots of Merton's Thought." *American Benedictine Review* 39:2 (June 1988) 178–87.

Hindman, Matthew. *The Myth of Digital Democracy*. Princeton: Princeton University Press, 2009.

Horan, Daniel, OFM. Striving Towards Authenticity: Merton's 'True Self' and the Millennial Generation's Search for Identity." *Merton Annual* 23 (2010) 80–89.

Hotz, Robert Lee. "As Brains Change So Can IQ, Study Finds Teens Brains May be More Malleable Than Thought," *The Wall Street Journal* (October 20, 2011) A 3.

Immordino-Yang, Mary Helen, et al. "Neural Correlates of Admiration and Compassion." *Proceedings of the National Academy of Sciences* 106 (May 12, 2009): 8021–26.

Inchausti, Robert. *Thomas Merton's American Prophecy*. Albany: State University of New York Press, 1998.

Internet World Stats Usage and Population Statistics, "Internet Usage Statistics" http://www.internetworldstats.com/stats.htm.

Isaacson, Walter. "In Search of the Real Bill Gates." *Time* (January 13, 1997). Online: http://www.time.com/time/magazine/article/0,9171,1120657,00.html.

Ishiguro, Kazuo. *Never Let Me Go.* New York: Vintage, 2005.

Jackson, Maggie. *Distracted: The Erosion of Attention and the Coming Dark Age.* Amherst, NY: Prometheus, 2008.

Jacoby, Susan. *The Age of American Unreason.* New York: Pantheon, 2008.

John Paul II. "Dangers of Genetic Manipulation." *L'Osservatore Romano* (December 5, 1983): 10–11.

Johnson, Karl E. "How Shall We Then Rest?" Online: http://www.booksandculture.com/articles/2010/julaug/shallwethenrest.html?paging=off.

Jones, James H. *Bad Blood: The Tuskegee Syphilis Experiment.* New York: Free Press, 1993.

Joy, Bill. "Why the Future Doesn't Need Us." *Wired* 8.04 (April, 2000). Online: http://www.wired.com/wired/archive/8.04/joy.html.

"Just Two in Five Americans Read a Newspaper Almost Every Day." (January 13, 2010.) Online: www.harrisinteractive.com/vault/Harris_Interactive_Poll_Media_Newspaper_Readers_2 010_01.pdf.

Kalathil, Shanti and Taylor C. Boas. *Open Networks, Closed Regimes: The Impact of the Internet on Authoritarian Rule.* Washinton, DC: Carnegie Endowment, 2003.

Kandel, Eric R. *In Search of Memory: The Emergence of a New Science of Mind.* New York: Norton, 2006.

Keen, Andrew. *The Cult of the Amateur: How Today's Internet Is Killing Our Culture and Assaulting Our Economy.* London: Brealey, 2006.

Keizer, Garrett. *The Unwanted Sound of Everything We Want: A Book About Noise.* New York: PublicAffairs, 2010.

Kelly, Frederic Joseph, S.J. *The Social Dimension of Religious Man in the Writings of Thomas Merton.* PhD diss., Catholic University of America, 1972.

Kelly, Kevin. "We Are the Web." *Wired* 13.08 (2005). Online: http://www.wired.com/wired/archive/13.08/tech.html.

King, Thomas. "Thomas Merton on Pierre Teilhard de Chardin." *The Merton Seasonal* 4 (Summer 1979) 2–4.

Kirp, David L. "After the Bell Curve: New Research Strengthens the Case Against Genetic Determinism," *The New York Times Magazine* (July 23, 2006) 15–19.

Klingberg, Torkel. *The Overflowing Brain: Information Overload and the Limits of Working Memory.* Oxford: Oxford University Press, 2009.

Koepp, M.J., "Evidence for Striatal Dopamine Release During a Video Game." *Nature* 393 (1998) 266–68.

Kropf, Richard W. "Crying With A Live Grief: The Mysticism of Merton and Teilhard Compared." *The Merton Annual* 5 (1992) 243–62.

Kurzweil, Ray. *The Age of Spiritual Machines: When Computers Exceed Human Intelligence.* New York: Viking, 1999.

———. *The Singularity Is Near.* New York: Viking, 2005.

Kurzweil, Raymond and Terry Grossman, MD. *Fantastic Voyage: Live Long Enough to Live Forever.* New York: Rodale, 2004.

———. *Transcend: Nine Steps to Living Forever.* New York: Rodale, 2009.

Labrie, Ross. *The Art of Thomas Merton.* Fort Worth: Texas Christian University Press, 1979.

Bibliography

Labrie, Ross. *Thomas Merton and the Inclusive Imagination*. Columbia, MO: University of Missouri, 2001.

Leahy, William K. and Anthony T. Massimini, eds. *Third Session Council Speeches of Vatican II*. Glen Rock, NJ: Deus, 1966.

Lehrer, Jonah. "The Forgetting Pill: How a Drug Can Target Your Worst Memories and Erase Them Forever," *Wired* (March 2012) 83–94, 120.

Lenhart, Amanda. *Cell Phones and American Adults*. Washington: Pew Research Center, 2010.

Levy, David. *Love and Sex With Robots: The Evolution of Human-Robot Relationships*. New York: Harper, 2007.

Lewin, Tamar. "If Your Kids Are Awake They're Probably Online." *New York Times* (January 20, 2010). Online: http://www.nytimes.com/2010/01/20/education/20wired.html.

Lewis, Gloria Kitto. "Thomas Merton's Myth for Modern Times." *The Merton Seasonal* 13 (Spring 1988) 10–15.

Ling, Rich. *New Tech, New Ties*. Boston: MIT Press, 2008.

Lohr, Steve. "Slow Down Brave Multitasker, and Don't Read This in Traffic." *New York Times* (March 25, 2007). Online: http://www.nytimes.com/2007/03/25/business/25multi.html.

Martin, James, SJ. "Status Update." *America* (June 4–11, 2011) 13–16.

Martin, Richard. "Mind Control." *Wired* 13.03 (March 2005). Online: http://www.wired.com/wired/archive/13.03/brain.html.

Marty, Martin E. "Creative Misuses of Jacques Ellul." In *Jacques Ellul: Interpretive Essays*, edited by Clifford G. Christians and Jay M. Van Hook, 3–16. Urbana: University of Illinois Press, 1981.

McLuhan, Marshall. *Understanding Media: The Extensions of Man*. New York: McGraw-Hill, 1964.

McPherson, Miller, et al. "Social Isolation in America: Changes in Core Discussion Networks over Two Decades." *American Sociological Review* 71 (June, 2006) 353–75.

"Merton and Basket Weaving." *The Merton Seasonal* 2 (Fall 1977) 10.

Merton, Thomas. "The Angel and the Machine." *The Merton Seasonal* 22 (Spring 1997) 3–6.

———. "Answers for Hernan Lavin Cerda." *The Merton Annual* 2 (1989) 3–12.

———. "The Answers of Minerva: Pacifism and Resistance in Simone Weil." In *The Literary Essays of Thomas Merton*, edited by Patrick Hart, 124–39. New York: New Directions, 1981.

———. *The Asian Journals of Thomas Merton*. New York: New Directions, 1968.

———. *The Behavior of Titans*. New York: New Directions, 1961.

———. "Blake and the New Theology." *Sewanee Review* 76 (October-December 1968): 673–82.

———. "A Buyer's Market for Love." *Ave Maria* 104 (December 24, 1966): 7–10.

———. *Cables to the Ace*. New York: New Directions, 1968.

———. *Choosing to Love the World: On Contemplation*. Edited by Jonathan Montaldo. Estes Park, CO: Sounds True, 2008.

———. "The Christian in a Technological World" (Electronic Paperback).

———. "The Church and the 'Godless World'-1." *The Merton Seasonal* 27 (Spring 2002) 7–8.

———. "The Church and the 'Godless World'-3." *The Merton Seasonal* 27 (Summer 2002) 3-7.

———. "The Church and the 'Godless World'-4." *The Merton Seasonal* 27 (Spring 2002) 3-9.

———. *The Collected Poems of Thomas Merton*. New York: New Directions, 1977.

———. *Conjectures of a Guilty Bystander*. New York: Doubleday, 1966.

———. "Contemplation and Action." In Thomas Merton, *On Nuclear Weapons*, 116-38. Chicago: Loyola University Press, 1988.

———. "The Contemplative Life in the Modern World." In Thomas Merton, *Faith and Violence*, 215-24. Notre Dame: University of Notre Dame Press, 1968.

———. *Contemplative Prayer*. New York: Image, 1971.

———. *The Courage for Truth*. Edited by Christine M. Bochen. New York: Farrar, Straus & Giroux, 1993.

———. *Dancing in the Water of Life*. Edited by Robert E. Daggy. San Francisco: Harper Collins, 1997.

———. *Day of a Stranger*. Salt Lake City: Smith, 1981.

———. *Disputed Questions*. New York: Harcourt Brace Jovanovich, 1960.

———. "Elegy for Ernest Hemingway." *Commonweal* 75 (September 22, 1961) 37-38.

———. *Entering the Silence*. Edited by Jonathan Montaldo. San Francisco: Harper-Collins, 1996.

———. "Events and Pseudo-Events Letter to a Southern Churchman." In Thomas Merton, *Faith and Violence*, 145-64. Notre Dame: University of Notre Dame Press, 1968.

———. *Faith and Violence*. Notre Dame: University of Notre Dame Press, 1968.

———. "Few Questions, Fewer Answers." *Harpers* 231 (1965) 79-81.

———. "First and Last Thoughts." In *A Thomas Merton Reader*, edited by Thomas P. McDonnell, 13-26. New York: Harcourt, Brace & World, 1974.

———. "Foreword." In *Saint Bernard of Clairvaux Seen Through his Selected Letters*, edited by Bruno Scott James, v-viii. Chicago: Regnery, 1953.

———. "Hagia Sophia." In Thomas Merton, *The Collected Poems of Thomas Merton*, 363-71. New York: New Directions, 1977.

———. *The Hidden Ground of Love*. Edited by William H. Shannon. New York: Farrar, Straus & Giroux, 1985.

———. "Huxley and the Ethics of Peace." In Thomas Merton, *The Literary Essays of Thomas Merton*, edited by Brother Patrick Hart, OCSO, 257-61. New York: New Directions, 1981.

———. *The Inner Experience*. New York: Harper Collins, 2003.

———. "Introduction." In *Religion in Wood*, edited by Edward D. Andrews and Faith Andrews, vii-xv. Bloomington: Indiana University Press, 1966.

———. *An Introduction to Christian Mysticism*. Kalamazoo, MI: Cistercian Publications, 2008.

———. "Is the World a Problem?" *Commonweal* 84 (June 3, 1966) 305.

———. *Learning to Love*. Edited by Christine M. Bochen. San Francisco: Harper-Collins, 1967.

———. "Lectio Divina." *Merton Collected Essays* 23 (Louisville: Thomas Merton Center) 55-95.

———. "Letter to the Editor." *Center Magazine* 4 (1968) 7.

Bibliography

———. "Letter to Pablo Antonio Cuadra." In Thomas Merton, *The Collected Poems of Thomas Merton*, 372–91. New York: New Directions, 1977.

———. *The Literary Essays of Thomas Merton*. Edited by Patrick Hart, OCSO. New York: New Directions, 1981.

———. *Love and Living*. Edited by Naomi Burton Stone and Brother Patrick Hart, OCSO. New York: Farrar, Straus & Giroux, 1979.

———. *Monastic Observances: Initiation into the Monastic Tradition*. Trappist, KY: Cistercian Publications, 2010.

———. *Mystics and Zen Masters*. New York: Farrar, Straus, & Giroux, 1967.

———. *The New Man*. Farrar, Straus & Cudahy, 1961.

———. *New Seeds of Contemplation*. New York: New Directions, 1961.

———. *No Man Is an Island*. New York: Harcourt Brace & Co., 1955.

———. *The Nonviolent Alternative*. New York: Farrar, Straus & Giroux, 1971.

———. *Original Child Bomb*. New York: New Directions, 1977.

———. "The Other Side of Despair." In Thomas Merton, *Mystics of Zen Masters*, 217–37. New York: Farrar, Straus & Giroux, 1967.

———. *Peace in the Post-Christian Era*. Maryknoll, NY: Orbis, 2004.

———. "The Plague of Camus: An Introduction." In Thomas Merton, *The Literary Essays of Thomas Merton*, edited by Patrick Hart, OCSO, 214–17. New York: New Directions, 1981.

———. *Praying the Psalms*. Collegeville, MN: Liturgical, 1956.

———. *Raids on the Unspeakable*. New York: New Directions, 1966.

———. *Rain and the Rhinoceros*. New York: New Directions, 1966.

———. Review of *In Tune with the World*, by Josef Pieper. *Cistercian Studies Quarterly* 1 (1966) 108–9.

———. *The Road to Joy*. Edited by Robert Daggy. New York: Farrar, Straus & Giroux, 1989.

———. *Run to the Mountain*. Edited by Patrick Hart, OCSO. San Francisco: Harper-Collins, 1995.

———. *The School of Charity*. Edited by Patrick Hart, OCSO. New York: Farrar, Straus & Giroux, 1990.

———. *A Search for Solitude*. Edited by Lawrence S. Cunningham. San Francisco: Harper-Collins, 1996.

———. *Seeking Paradise: The Spirit of the Shakers*. Edited by Paul Pearson. Maryknoll, NY: Orbis, 2003.

———. *Seven Story Mountain*. New York: Harcourt, Brace & Co., 1948.

———. "The Shakers." *Jubilee* 11:9 (January 1964) 37–41.

———. *The Sign of Jonas*. New York: Harcourt, Brace & Co., 1953.

———. *Spiritual Direction and Meditation*. Collegeville, MN: Liturgical, 1960.

———. "Technology." *Merton Collected Essays*, vol. 6, 53–59. Louisville: Thomas Merton Center, Bellarmine College, 1967.

———. "Teilhard's Gamble: Betting on the Whole Human Species." *Commonweal* 87 (October 27, 1967) 109–11.

———. *Thomas Merton in Alaska*. New York: New Directions, 1988.

———. *Thoughts in Solitude*. Boston: Shambala, 1956.

———. *Turning Toward the World*. Edited by Victor A. Kramer. San Francisco: Harper-Collins, 1996.

———. "Una Sociedad que Esta Peligrosamente Enferma." 2 *Punto Final* (August 1967) 12–14.

———. *The Way of Chuang Tzu.* New York: New Directions, 1965.

———. *When the Trees Say Nothing.* Edited by Kathleen Deignan. Notre Dame: University of Notre Dame Press, 2003.

———. "The Wild Places." *The Catholic Worker* 34 (July-August 1967) 4–6.

———. "Wilderness and Paradise." *Cistercian Studies* 2 (November 1966) 83–89.

———. *The Wisdom of the Desert.* New York: New Directions, 1960.

———. *Witness to Freedom.* Edited by William H. Shannon. New York: Harcourt Brace & Co., 1994.

———. *Zen and the Birds of Appetite.* New York: New Directions, 1968.

Merton, Thomas and Jean Leclercq. *Survival or Prophecy? The Letters of Thomas Merton and Jean Leclercq.* Edited by Brother Patrick Hart, OCSO. New York: Farrar, Straus & Giroux, 2002.

Merton, Thomas and Rosemary Radford Reuther. *At Home in the World: The Letters of Thomas Merton and Rosemary Radford Reuther.* Edited by Mary Tardiff. Maryknoll, NY: Orbis, 1995.

Metz, Steve. "Editor's Corner." *The Science Teacher* (October, 2006): 8.

Miller, Stephen. "Robert Ettinger: Pursuing Immortality He Followed Frozen Path." *The Wall Street Journal* (July 26, 2011) A8.

Morris, James and George Stone. "Children and Psychotropic Medication: A Cautionary Note." *Journal of Marital and Family Therapy* (December 17, 2009). Online: http:// DOI: 10.1111/j.1752–606.2009.00178.x.

Mossberg, Walter S. "If You Have ChaCha And a Cellphone You Have Answers." *The Wall Street Journal* (April 24, 2008) D1.

Mosteller, Timothy. "Aristotle and Headless Clones." *Theoretical Medicine and Bioethics* 26 (2005) 339–50

Mott, Michael. *The Seven Mountains of Thomas Merton.* New York: Harcourt Brace, 1993.

Naik, Gautam. "A Baby, Please. Blond, Freckles—Hold the Colic. Laboratory Techniques That Screen for Diseases in Embryos Are Now Being Offered to Create Designer Children." *The Wall Street Journal* (February 12, 2009) A 10

———. "Mice Are Created From Two Males." *The Wall Street Journal* (December 10, 2010) A 8.

———. "Scientists Build a Rat Lung in a Lab." *The Wall Street Journal* (June 25, 2010) A 3.

Nash, Roderick. *Wilderness and the American Mind.* New Haven, CT: Yale University Press, 1967.

Nass, Clifford. *The Man Who Lied to His Laptop.* New York: Current, 2010.

National Conference on Catholic Bishops. *Religion, Science, and the Search for Wisdom.* Washington: USCC, 1987.

National Endowment for the Arts. *To Read or Not to Read.* Washington, DC, 2007.

National Geographic Society. "Merging Man and Machine." *National Geographic* (January, 2010).

National Science Foundation and Department of Commerce. *Converging Technologies for Improving Human Performance.* Arlington, VA: 2002.

Nemesszeghy, E. and J. Russell. *The Theology of Evolution.* Notre Dame, IN: Fides, 1971.

Padovano, Anthony D. *The Human Journey.* New York: Doubleday, 1982.

Bibliography

Pennington, Basil, ed. *Toward an Integrated Humanity: Thomas Merton's Journey*. Kalamazoo, MI: Cistercian Publications, 1987.

Pernick, Martin S. *The Black Stork: Eugenics and the Death of "Defective" Babies in American Medicine and Motion Pictures Since 1915*. Oxford: Oxford University Press, 1996.

Planck, Max. *Where Is Science Going?* New York: Norton, 1932.

Plato, *Phaedrus*. Fairfield, IA: World Library, 2008.

Plotz, David. *The Genius Factory*. New York: Random House, 2005.

Poole, Michael. "A Critique of Aspects of the Philosophy and Theology of Richard Dawkins." *Science and Christian Belief* 6 (1995) 41–59.

———. "A Response to Dawkins." *Science and Christian Belief* 7 (1995) 51–58.

Postman, Neil. *Amusing Ourselves to Death*. New York: Penguin, 1986.

Potter, Steven. *Designer Genes*. New York: Random House, 2010.

Powaski, Ronald E. *Thomas Merton on Nuclear Weapons*. Chicago: Loyola University Press, 1988.

Pramuk, Christopher. *Sophia: The Hidden Idea of Thomas Merton*. Collegeville, MN: Liturgical, 2009.

President's Council on Bioethics. *Beyond Therapy: Biotechnology and the Pursuit of Happiness*. New York: Harper Collins, 2003.

Price, Geoffrey. "The Nuclear Issue and Human Sciences." In *Religion and Culture: Essays in Honor of Bernard Lonergan, SJ*, edited by Timothy P. Fallon and Philip Boo Riley, 277–93. Albany: State University of New York Press, 1987.

Prochnik, George. *In Pursuit of Silence, Listening for Meaning in a World of Noise*. New York: Doubleday, 2010.

Putnam, Robert. *Bowling Alone*. New York: Simon and Schuster, 2001.

Ratzinger, Cardinal Joseph. "Preface." In *Evolutionismus und Christentum*, edited by R. Spaemann, et al., vii–ix. Weinheim: 1986.

Reardon, Marguerite. "U.S Text Usage Hits Record Despite Price Increases." (2008.) Online: http://news.cnet.com/8301-1035_3-10038634-94.html.

Rice, Alexandra. "Bleary Eyed Students Can't Stop Texting Even to Sleep, a Researcher Finds," *Chronicle of Higher Education* (November 25, 2011) A13.

Richtel, Matt. "Attached to Technology and Paying a Price," *New York Times* (June 6, 2010). Online: http://www.nytimes.com/2010/06/07/technology/07brain.html.

———. "Growing Up Digital, Wired for Distraction," *New York Times* (November 21, 2010) A1.

———. "In Classroom of the Future, Stagnant Scores," *New York Times* (September 4, 2011) A1.

———. "Thou Shall Not Kill, Except in a Game at Church," *New York Times* (October 7, 2007) A1, A20.

Richtel, Matt and Miguel Helft. "Facebook Users Who Are Under Age Raise Concerns," *New York Times* (March 11, 2011). Online: http://www.nytimes.com/2011/03/12/technology/internet/12underage.html.

Rickover, Hyman. "A Humanistic Technology." *American Behavioral Scientist* 9, No. 1, (1965) 3–8.

Ridley, Matt. "Why Things Can't Get Better Faster (or Slower)?" *The Wall Street Journal* (October 20–21, 2012), C4.

Rochelle, J. M., et al., "Changing How and What Children Learn in School with Computer-Based Technologies." *Children and Computer Technology* 10:2 (2000) 76–101.

Rops, Daniel. *Edouard Le Roy et son fauteil.* Paris: Fayard, 1956.

Rosen, Christine. "Everyone is Talking." Review of *New Tech, New Ties: How Mobile Communication is Reshaping Social Cohesion,* by Richard Ling, *The Wall Street Journal* (April 28, 2008): A15.

Rosen, Christine. *Preaching Eugenics.* New York: Oxford University Press, 2004.

Rowland, Tracy. *Culture and the Thomist Tradition.* New York: Routledge, 2003.

Roy, David J., M.D. "Bioethics as Anamnesis." In *Creativity and Method: Essays in Honor of Bernard Lonergan,* edited by Matthew Lamb, 325–28. Milwaukee, WI: Marquette University, 1981.

———. "The Severely Defective Newborn." In *Health and Christian Life,* 18–28. Ottawa: Catholic Health Association of Canada, 1978.

Ruse, Michael. "Confirmation and Falsification of Theories of Evolution." *Scientia* 104 (1988) 329–57.

Russell, Robert John, et al., *Neuroscience and the Person: Scientific Perspectives on Divine Action.* Vatican: Vatican Observatory Publications, 1999.

Ryan, Greg. "Thomas Merton—Computer Hacker (A Cyber Fantasy)." *The Merton Seasonal* 23 (Spring 1998) 8–13.

Sacred Congregation for the Doctrine of the Faith. "Euthanasia." *The Pope Speaks* 25 (Winter 1980) 290–98.

Sagan, Scott. *The Limits of Safety: Organizations, Accidents and Nuclear Weapons.* Princeton: Princeton University Press, 1995.

Sacred Congregation for the Doctrine of the Faith. *Instruction on Respect for Human Life in Its Origin and in the Dignity of Procreation.* Washington: USCC, 1987.

Shannon, William. "Can One Be a Contemplative in a Technological Society?" *The Merton Seasonal* 22 (Spring 1997) 12–20.

———. "Christian Living in an Age of Technology." In *Toward an Integrated Humanity,* edited by Basil Pennington, 179–90. Kalamazoo, MI: Cistercian Publications, 1987.

———. "The Year of the Cold War Letters." In *Toward an Integrated Humanity: Thomas Merton's Journey,* edited by Basil M. Pennington, 166–71. Kalamazoo, MI: Cistercian Publications, 1987.

Shattuck, Roger. *Forbidden Knowledge.* New York: Harcourt Brace, Jovanovich, 1996.

Shermer, Michael. "Defying the Doomsayers," *The Wall Street Journal* (February 22, 2012) A 13.

Shields, M. K. and R. E. Behrman. "Children and Computer Technology: Analysis and Recommendations." *The Future of Children* 10:2 (2000) 4–30.

Shirky, Clay. *Cognitive Surplus.* New York: Penguin, 2010.

———. *Here Comes Everybody: The Power of Organizing Without Organizations.* New York: Penguin, 2009.

Shulevitz, Judith. *The Sabbath World: Glimpses of a Different Order of Time.* New York: Random House, 2010.

Silver, Lee. *Remaking Eden: How Genetic Engineering and Cloning Will Change the American Family.* New York: Avon, 1998.

Small, Gary and Gigi Vorgan. *iBrain: Surviving the Technological Alteration of the Modern Mind.* New York: Collins, 2008.

Solomon, Deborah. "The Russian Immigrant's Handbook," *The New York Times Magazine* (July 18, 2010) 17.

Song, Felicia Wu. *Virtual Communities*. New York: Lang, 2009.

Spar, Debora L. *The Baby Business: How Money, Science and Politics Drive the Commerce of Conception*. Cambridge, MA: Harvard Business School Press, 2006.

Stein, Rob. "Fairfax clinic's giveaway of donor eggs sparks uproar," *Washington Post* (March 18, 2010) A1.

Steindl-Rast, David. "Man or Prayer." In *Thomas Merton, Monk: A Monastic Tribute*, edited by Patrick Hart, OCSO, 12–22. New York: Sheed & Ward, 1974.

Stevens, Alex, Kati Leslie, and Jeffrey Scott. "Mom Urges Execution," *Atlanta Journal Constitution* (December 8, 2011) A1, A18.

Stock, Gregory. *Redesigning Humans: Our Inevitable Genetic Future*. New York: Houghton Mifflin, 2002.

Stoll, Clifford. *High Tech Heretic: Reflections of a Computer Contrarian*. New York: Anchor, 2000.

Strom. Stephanie. "Charities Go Mobile in Appeal to Young," *New York Times* (June 25, 2011) B1, B4.

Szilard, Leo. "Letter to Thomas Merton." May 2, 1962, in Thomas Merton Collection at Bellarmine University, Louisville, Kentucky.

Tardiff, Mary, ed. *At Home in the World: The Letters of Thomas Merton and Rosemary Radford Reuther*. Maryknoll, NY: Orbis, 2005.

Taubman, Philip. *The Partnership: Five Cold Warriors and Their Quest to Ban the Bomb*. New York: Harper, 2012.

Thompson, Phillip M. *Between Science and Religion: The Engagement of Catholic Intellectuals with Science and Technology in the Twentieth Century*. Lanham, MD: Lexington, 2010.

———. "Seeking Common Ground in a World of Ethical Pluralism: A Review Essay of *Moral Acquaintances: Methodology in Bioethics* by Kevin M. Wildes, SJ." *HEC Forum* 16 (June 2004): 114–28.

———. "Silent Protest: A Catholic Justice Dissents in *Buck v. Bell*." *The Catholic Lawyer* 43 (2004) 125–48.

Tierney, John. "To Choose is to Lose," *The New York Times Magazine* (August 21, 2011) 34–46.

Turkle, Sherry. *Alone Together*. New York: Basic, 2011.

Wang, Shirley S. "Cell Study Finds a Way to Slow the Ravages of Age," *The Wall Street Journal* (November 3, 2011) A2.

———. "Closing in on the Formula for Artificial Skin," *The Wall Street Journal* (July 6, 2010) D3.

Warren, Luigi, et al., "Highly Efficient Reprogramming to Pluripotency and Directed Differentiation of Human Cells with Synthetic Modified mRNA." *Cell Stem Cell* 7 (November 5, 2010) 1–13.

Weikart, Richard. *From Darwin to Hitler: Evolutionary Ethics, Eugenics, and Racism in Germany*. New York: Palgrave Macmillan, 2004.

Weiner, Jonathan. *Long for this World*. New York: Harper Collins, 2010.

Weintraub, Arlene. *Selling the Fountain of Youth*. New York: Basic, 2010.

Weis, Monica. "Dancing with the Raven, Thomas Merton's Evolving View of Nature." In *The Vision of Thomas Merton*, edited by Patrick O'Connell, 135–53. Notre Dame, IN: Ave Maria, 2003.

Weis, Monica. "Living Beings Call Us to Reflective Living: Mary Austin, Thomas Merton and Contemporary Nature Writers." *The Merton Seasonal* 17 (Autumn 1992) 4–9.

Weiss, Rick. "Human Brain Cells Grow in Mice," *Washington Post* (December 13, 2005). Online: http://www.washingtonpost.com/wpdyn/content/article/2005/12/12/AR2005121201388.html.

Weiss, Rick. "U.S. Denies Patent for a Too-Human Hybrid?" *Washington Post* (February 13, 2005) A3.

Wildes, Kevin. *Moral Acquaintances*. Notre Dame: University of Notre Dame Press, 1994.

Wolf, Maryanne. *Proust and the Squid: The Story of Science and the Reading Brain*. New York: Harper, 2007.

Wu, John, Jr. "Technological Perspectives: Thomas Merton and the One-Eyed Giant." *Merton Annual* 13 (2000) 80–104.

Wynn, Wilton. *Keepers of the Keys*. New York: Random House, 1988.

Zachary, Paul. "Is the Key to Creativity in Your Pillbox or in Your PC?" *New York Times* (March 18, 2007) B3

Zimmerman, Eilene. "Distracted: It's Time to Hit the Reset Button," *New York Times* (November 20, 2011) B8.

Zito, J. et. al., "Psychotropic Patterns for Youth: A Ten Year Perspective." *Archives of Pediatric and Adolescent Medicine* 157 (2003) 17–25.

Index

Returning to Reality

Returning to Reality